THE ESSENTIALS

Supporting Young Children
with Disabilities in the Classroom

THE ESSENTIALS

Supporting Young Children with Disabilities in the Classroom

Pamela Brillante

National Association for the Education of Young Children
Washington, DC

National Association for the
Education of Young Children
1313 L Street NW, Suite 500
Washington, DC 20005-4101
202-232-8777 • 800-424-2460
NAEYC.org

NAEYC Books

Senior Director, Content Strategy
and Development
Susan Friedman

Editor-in-Chief
Kathy Charner

Senior Creative Design Manager
Audra Meckstroth

Senior Editor
Holly Bohart

Publishing Manager
Francine Markowitz

Creative Design Specialist
Malini Dominey

Associate Editor
Rossella Procopio

Through its publications program,
the National Association for the
Education of Young Children
(NAEYC) provides a forum for
discussion of major issues and
ideas in the early childhood
field, with the hope of provoking
thought and promoting
professional growth. The views
expressed or implied in this book
are not necessarily those of the
Association.

NAEYC would like to thank the staff and children of National
Children's Center in Washington, DC, and of The Campus
School at Boston College. Photos from these centers appear
throughout this book.

Photo credits

Copyright © NAEYC: xi, 3 (left), 9 (left), 21, 25 (both), 33 (left),
37, 43 (right), 51 (right), 61 (right), 63 (right), 71 (left), 85 (right),
93, 101 (both), 103, 121, 123 (right), 127, 131, and 142

Copyright © The Campus School at Boston College: 33 (right),
43 (left), 57, and 89 (right)

Copyright © iStock: viii, 3 (right), 6, 9 (right), 51 (left), 52, 61
(left), 63 (left), 67, 71 (right), 73 (both), 77 (both), 83 (both),
85 (left), 89 (left), 99, 104, 107, 109, 113 (both), 119 (both),
and 123 (left)

Library of Congress Control Number: 2017933147

ISBN: 978-1-938113-29-1

Item 1131

Contents

Disabilities and Young Children

Specific Disabilities

About the Book

Chances are, at some point in your early childhood career, you will work with children who have, or might have, a developmental delay or disability, along with their families. This book offers essential information about disabilities and how they impact young children's learning and development. More than that, it encourages you to go beyond a child's disability label to see her strengths, needs, interests, and preferences and to figure out how best to support those in the classroom, just as you do for any other child. Regardless of medical diagnoses or individual challenges, children with disabilities are first and foremost children.

Who Is This Book For?

This book is a resource for early childhood educators and preservice teachers who work or will work with children birth through age 8 who have developmental delays or disabilities. Young children with delays or disabilities are educated in many different settings, including public and private preschools, child care centers, family child care programs, the child's home, general education classrooms in elementary schools, and programs specifically designed to educate students with disabilities. With a foundation of developmentally appropriate practices and supports for children, their families, and educators as well, all of these settings can be effective learning environments.

Program directors and administrators as well as providers of physical, occupational, and speech-language therapy will also find the information in this book useful as they work with teachers and families to help children become active participants in their environments and master a variety of skills.

Language and Words Matter

Words help us express our understanding of and feelings about people, things, ideas, and experiences. They are a powerful tool that can influence and change perspectives and opinions. This book will help you understand more about disabilities and their implications for children and families, and this knowledge, along with your understanding of children in general, will help you recognize and rebut inaccurate or harmful stereotypes and attitudes about individuals with disabilities.

In an effort to view young children with disabilities first as young children, this book uses **people-first language,** a way of referring to an individual with a disability that focuses on the person rather than the disability. For example, this book refers to *children with* *autism spectrum disorder* rather than *autistic children*. Shifting the focus from a single part of someone that others may view as different or deficient to the whole person with feelings, dignity, and rights is a reminder that everyone, no matter their ability or disability, is capable and deserving of respect.

While it is generally appropriate and respectful to use people-first language, keep in mind that some individuals or groups of individuals with disabilities prefer to use what is known as **identity-first language** to refer to themselves. For example, many people in the American Deaf community see their deafness as inseparable from who they are, and they prefer to be called *Deaf* rather than *a person who is deaf*. Respect each person's choice for what she wishes to be called or wishes her child to be called.

What Is in This Book?

Part 1, "Disabilities and Young Children," helps you relate what you already know about young children to those who have or may have a delay or disability; understand how laws relating to children with disabilities affect your day-to-day interactions with children and their families; navigate the process of identifying, assessing, and qualifying a child for services; understand the roles of individuals who provide services to a child; provide the general kind of environment, experiences, and teaching practices that children with disabilities need and deserve; and address challenging behaviors.

Part 2, "Specific Disabilities," discusses more in depth some particular disabilities young children may have and specific issues teachers often face when working with a child. It also offers practical strategies for providing support and intervention for children.

This book provides a brief overview of research-based information and strategies for working with children who have disabilities. To deepen your professional knowledge and help families who are looking for more information on how to support their child, see the resource list provided on pages 143–145.

Disabilities and Young Children

1 Different, Yet Alike

Alyssa is excited about her first teaching position in a Head Start classroom with fourteen 4-year-olds. While Alyssa is planning for her new class over the summer, Mrs. Helman, the center director, tells her that one of the children, Chloe, has spina bifida and uses crutches to walk. Alyssa remembers learning some things about special education in college, but she isn't confident that she knows enough to teach a child with a disability.

During the first few weeks of school, Alyssa spends a lot of time focused on Chloe. She watches every move Chloe makes around the classroom, concerned that she won't be able to keep up—or even worse, that she'll get knocked down by one of her classmates.

After the first few weeks, Alyssa relaxes a bit. Chloe is proficient at using her crutches to get around and keep up with the other children, and her cognitive skills are above average for her age. However, she has difficulty negotiating the playground, and this keeps her from fully joining her classmates in play. Alyssa determines to solve the playground issue.

Alyssa is also concerned about the development of a couple of the other children. Jamari easily follows the daily routines of the classroom and enjoys playing with several other boys, but his language skills seem to lag behind the other children's. Leo, a pleasant child who immerses himself in sensory activities like sand and water exploration, has difficulty remembering some of the basic math and language concepts that Alyssa focuses on throughout the day.

Alyssa is proud that all of the children are learning new skills, and she knows that providing developmentally appropriate experiences benefits Chloe, Jamari, and Leo in many ways, but she feels the need to do more for these three children. She just doesn't know where to start.

Nearly every early childhood educator has taught a child with a disability, but often the disability has not yet been identified. Children grow and develop at their own pace during the early childhood years, and many disabilities that impact learning start to become apparent but are not identified until later. Jamari and Leo, for example, show delays in particular areas at age 4, and each may or may not eventually be diagnosed with a disability. Early childhood educators are often the first professionals to suspect that there is a delay or a disability, and many times they are also the first to start interventions.

Even if a child has been identified as having a disability, she is first and foremost a child. And best practices for young children are best practices for *all* young children. All children thrive in programs with developmentally appropriate experiences and support for their individual strengths, interests, and needs. Chloe's disability, for example, impacts her in *some* ways but not in all, and participating in a high-quality early childhood classroom fosters her academic and social development—areas that are not affected by her disability. Considering Chloe's physical needs and how she can more fully participate with the other children will result in making the environment more accessible, giving her more opportunities for growth. Play and exploration, interaction with peers, and appropriate learning challenges are important for every child, opportunities that should not be limited or denied because of a disability or delay.

The Same Rights for All Children

Every child with a delay or a disability has the following rights:

The Right to High-Quality Programs

Children with delays or disabilities deserve the same high-quality education alongside their same-age peers who do not have a disability. Early childhood programs are often the first places children become engaged in group learning opportunities and social interactions with other children outside their homes. Many children with disabilities need specific adaptations to some routines and activities, and they may need more time to learn concepts and practice certain skills. In many ways, however, children with delays or disabilities have a great deal in common with every other child, and they deserve the same developmentally appropriate programs that are supported by research on how young children learn and develop.

The Right to Legal Protections Under the Law

Laws in the United States and many other countries provide rights and protections for children with delays or disabilities. The Individuals with Disabilities Education Act (IDEA) of 2004 (Public Law 108-446) was designed to help children with disabilities learn and participate in everyday routines and activities with their peers with the supports and services they need to be successful. IDEA also lists procedural safeguards that give families a voice in the educational decisions made for their children and protect their rights with regard to their children's education.

The Right to Be Part of the Community

Children with delays or disabilities deserve to be educated in schools and programs alongside their same-age peers. Removing children from programs due to their challenging behaviors (without looking at what those behaviors are communicating) or segregating children into special programs or schools violates a core value of a community's commitment to create programs that respect, value, and educate everyone.

The Right to Be Respected for Themselves

Children with delays or disabilities have a right to receive the individual attention and support they need to be successful. The effects of some disabilities may be lifelong, but children's needs can be addressed with the appropriate supports and services. Programs, educators, and families must make decisions about each child as an individual and ensure that educational policies and practices do not unnecessarily impede children's success.

Child Development, Delays, and Disabilities

Child development is commonly defined as the process children go through physically, intellectually, socially, and emotionally from birth until adolescence. Young children change, grow, and learn more during the first few years of life than they do at any other time. The brain uses the body as a tool to learn, and every time a child touches, hears, sees, smells, or tastes something new, her brain connects these actions to different concepts (Dotson-Renta 2016; UNICEF et al. 2010). When she has new experiences or encounters new situations, her body helps her brain interpret and bring meaning to these experiences by gathering information. As the brain makes these connections, children learn.

Developmental milestones
The Centers for Disease Control and Prevention (CDC) and the American Academy of Pediatrics (AAP) created a comprehensive list of expected developmental milestones from the age of 2 months through 5 years. This can be found at www.cdc.gov/ncbddd/actearly/milestones/index.html.

All children develop at their own pace. While no one can predict exactly when an individual child will develop certain skills, such as walking or talking, we have a general idea of when to expect these changes, referred to as developmental milestones.

Developmental Expectations

Understanding each area of a child's development and the expectations for development at each age is key to identifying a possible delay in development or a disability. Development tends to follow a general pattern, and some children may seem late in developing in one area or in several. Since many developmental milestones typically occur around a specific time in a child's life, some parents and teachers start to worry when those milestones are delayed or are not reached at all.

Childhood is a journey, not a race
This often-heard saying serves as a powerful reminder that while it is tempting to assume that reaching developmental milestones early—or ahead of peers—is desirable, that is not always the case. Children's development is not a competition, and it is very important to look at the overall development of a child, not just his development in one or two isolated areas.

Parents are naturally concerned about the development of their child and instinctively compare their child to a playmate or another child in the family. They want to know if their child is walking early enough or saying enough words at a certain age. Sometimes they are reassured by family and friends that many children who do not speak or walk until later than expected eventually do develop these skills. Even doctors may tell parents that their concerns are nothing to worry about at this time.

Teachers also become concerned about the development of some of the children they work with. Experiences with many children around the same age give teachers the opportunity to observe what the stages of development look like across many different children. With that knowledge, the teacher may be one of the first professionals to identify a potential delay or disability.

Developmental Delays

Developmental milestones give parents a general sense of when their child will develop skills like walking, talking, feeding herself, and becoming toilet trained. Children develop at their own pace, but pediatricians use these developmental milestones to make sure children are generally developing on schedule and to catch any delay in development as early as possible (CDC 2017b).

Doctors routinely look at a child's overall development as well as some specific developmental skills when they examine the child during regular office visits (CDC 2017a). Some of the common milestones doctors and families discuss during visits include

» **Motor development:** Is the child rolling over, sitting, or standing yet? Is he moving around by himself? How well does he use his fingers to manipulate small objects?

» **Language development:** How many words does the child say, and how clearly does she speak? How well does she understand what other people say to her?

» **Social and emotional development:** Does the child show interest in what is going on around her? Does she show a range of emotions and an increasing ability to regulate them? How does she interact with other children and adults?

» **Cognitive development:** Is the child curious? Does he explore toys and other materials in the environment? Does he understand cause and effect? Does he problem solve?

Again, developmental milestones are what *most* children can do at a certain age, but it is not an exact science. If a child develops a skill one month later than the developmental milestone chart indicates she should, that is usually not of concern. However, most doctors do become concerned if a child is several months behind. For example, most children start to walk unassisted between the ages of 9 months and 15 months. With this in mind, if a child is not walking at

» 16 or 17 months, that may be nothing serious to worry about, but the doctor will want to know about it.

» 18 or 19 months, that is of greater concern, and the doctor may want to look at the child's development even further.

» 20 months, that is a significant concern, and a doctor or specialist should complete a formal developmental evaluation.

When there is a significant delay in development, doctors identify children as having a **developmental delay**. A child may show a developmental delay in just one area of development, or the delay can impact more than one area. A **global developmental delay** indicates a delay in at least two areas of development (AAP 2006).

Possible Causes for Developmental Delays

There are a number of reasons why developmental delays occur. A child may be born prematurely, or there could be an underlying genetic condition. In many situations, doctors and families do not know the specific cause.

Temporary conditions that can cause developmental delays. A delay in a child's development might be due to a temporary condition. For example, ongoing or recurrent ear infections in young children can cause short-term hearing loss, leading to delays in speech and language (ASHA 2017a). Infections in the inner ear may also cause balance problems in young children and delay walking (Lawson 2015). When a developmental delay is caused by a temporary condition that can be resolved with time and medical interventions such as therapy, most children make significant improvements when treatment begins as early as possible.

Child Development Expectations Across Cultures

Families from all cultures want their children to learn and develop, but different cultures have different expectations and prioritize certain aspects of development over others. Considering the culture of each child and family is important when looking for specific milestones. What may look like a delay in language or social skills may be considered typical or even preferred development in some cultures.

For example, children in European, American, and other Western cultures are often expected to be independent as soon as possible. Other cultures, including Asian or Eastern cultures, often value interdependence, cooperation, and other skills that are important to being part of a group (Basu-Zharku 2011; Chen 2009). These diverse cultural expectations may result in a variety of social interactions and behaviors in classrooms. For example, children from a culture such as China tend to act less aggressively in group situations than children from Western cultures, like the United States (Rubin & Menzer 2010).

Other common early childhood experiences are also influenced by culture. Pretend play, for example, is not common in some Eastern countries like Korea, and when it does occur, a child is more likely to pretend to be a family member than a community helper, fairy-tale character, or action hero, which are common roles seen among children from Western cultures (Chen 2009).

Disabilities that can cause developmental delays. Often a delay in development is due to a disability, either known or not yet identified. Developmental delays can result from long-term medical conditions, such as

- » Genetic disorders (Down syndrome, Tay-Sachs disease)
- » Neurological disorders (muscular dystrophy)
- » Trauma occurring before, during, or soon after birth (cerebral palsy) (CDC 2015a)

Some disabilities that are likely to cause developmental delays are identified at birth or even before, such as Down syndrome. In other situations, the cause for the developmental delay may be a disability that cannot be identified at a young age but is eventually diagnosed when a child is older. Such conditions include autism spectrum disorder (ASD) and attention-deficit/hyperactivity disorder (ADHD) (CDC 2015a).

When a developmental delay is caused by a disability, the delay usually continues throughout the person's lifetime. Special education and related services that begin as early as possible are crucial for enhancing children's development and learning.

Developmental Disabilities

The Americans with Disabilities Act (ADA) of 1990 (Public Law 101-336) defines a **disability** as a physical or mental condition that impacts the way the body works or develops, and significantly limits a person's abilities in one or more major life activities, including walking, standing, seeing, hearing, speaking, and/or learning.

More specifically, the Developmental Disabilities Assistance and Bill of Rights Act of 2000 (Public Law 106-402) defines a **developmental disability** as a severe, chronic disability that

» Originates at birth or during childhood

» Is attributable to a mental or physical impairment or a combination of mental and physical impairments

» Is expected to continue indefinitely

» Substantially restricts the individual's functioning in three or more of the following major life activities:

- Self-care

- Receptive and expressive language

- Learning

- Mobility

- Self-direction

- Capacity for independent living

- Economic self-sufficiency

Some examples of developmental disabilities are Down syndrome, cerebral palsy, fetal alcohol spectrum disorder, spina bifida, and brain injury.

Developmental disabilities have a high probability of impacting a child's achievement of developmental milestones, so it is important that services such as special education and related services such as speech-language therapy begin as early as possible. Children with developmental disabilities may be eligible for supports and services even before the condition affects their development. For example, since it is probable that a child born with spina bifida will have difficulty with motor development (crawling and walking), he should be eligible for physical therapy from the early intervention system (see Chapter 2) even before he is expected to start crawling or walking.

Suspecting a Delay or Disability

Parents are often the first to notice that their child is not progressing at the same rate as other children the same age. In some cases, a teacher might notice a child's delay, or a pediatrician might detect a medical issue during a regularly scheduled checkup. If parents think their child is developing a little slowly in an area or if he seems behind in development, it is essential to talk to a medical doctor. If a child continually lags behind in skills other children his age have acquired, it is time to assess the cause. Ongoing, significant delays in achieving developmental milestones may signal a disability.

2 Identifying the Needs of Young Children with Disabilities

Ensuring that young children with delays and disabilities are identified and given the same opportunities to succeed as their peers without disabilities is a goal that encompasses numerous entities, including public and private schools, hospitals, and even the US government.

The federal government recognizes that many individuals with disabilities, including young children, face discrimination and barriers that make being included as members of their community almost impossible. The Americans with Disabilities Act (ADA), passed in 1990 and reauthorized in 2009, sets out to break down these barriers and guarantee that all people with disabilities can participate in American society.

Title III of the ADA prohibits child care providers from denying admission, terminating enrollment, or in any way discriminating against or excluding a child from a program because of a disability. The ADA also says that programs must make reasonable adaptations when necessary in order to accommodate the individual needs of each child (Child Care Law Center 2011).

Education laws, including specific special education laws, go beyond a child's right to access educational programs and address how to meet the educational needs of children with disabilities so they can develop to their full potential.

Education for All Handicapped Children Act

In 1975, with the passage of the Education for All Handicapped Children Act (Public Law 94-142), the US government outlined the educational rights of children with disabilities and their families and allocated funds to states to provide children a free, appropriate public education and related services. Initially the law applied only to children and adults ages 3 through 21; those under the age of 3 were not eligible.

Amended in 1986 as Public Law 99-457, the law recognized the need to provide intervention services to infants and toddlers (from birth through age 2) who had a

developmental delay or a diagnosed condition with a high probability of leading to a developmental delay. Provision of services for these children and their families was mandated, and states were given the option of providing services for infants and toddlers who were at risk for having a delay due to conditions such as low birth weight and abuse or neglect (Center for Parent Information and Resources 2014a).

Individuals with Disabilities Education Act

In 2004, the law was reauthorized and renamed the Individuals with Disabilities Education Act (IDEA) (Public Law 108-446). In 2011, the final set of regulations for Part C of IDEA, which pertained to infants and toddlers, was published. These regulations help states interpret the intentions of IDEA Part C and provide guidance for developing programs for infants and toddlers with delays or disabilities.

Part B of IDEA covers children and adults ages 3 through 21. Since services are administered differently under these two sections of the law, the processes of evaluating and providing services for infants and toddlers and for older children are discussed separately in this chapter.

Early Intervention: Birth Through Age 2

Early intervention is a system of services for infants and toddlers with developmental delays or disabilities and their families. Early intervention providers do not just work with the child; they also work closely with the family to support their child during everyday routines and activities.

Each state administers its own early intervention program, so procedures for obtaining assistance, timelines for the steps in the process, and terminology vary from state to state and may even change over time. However, the basic steps outlined by the federal government are similar. These are discussed below and outlined in the figure shown here, "Individualized Family Service Plan (IFSP) Process."

The Early Intervention Referral and Evaluation Process

1. Contacting the community early intervention system

In some states, the Department of Education and public schools coordinate the early intervention system, while in other states it is the Department of Health or another agency. To obtain contact information for early intervention services in their community, families can contact any medical doctor who treats infants and toddlers, such as a doctor in a local clinic or the pediatric department at a local hospital. Local public schools also may have

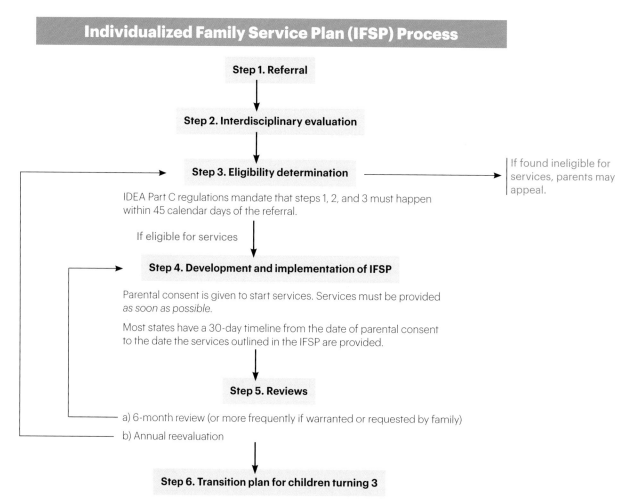

Individualized Family Service Plan (IFSP) Process

Step 1. Referral

Step 2. Interdisciplinary evaluation

Step 3. Eligibility determination

If found ineligible for services, parents may appeal.

IDEA Part C regulations mandate that steps 1, 2, and 3 must happen within 45 calendar days of the referral.

If eligible for services

Step 4. Development and implementation of IFSP

Parental consent is given to start services. Services must be provided *as soon as possible.*

Most states have a 30-day timeline from the date of parental consent to the date the services outlined in the IFSP are provided.

Step 5. Reviews

a) 6-month review (or more frequently if warranted or requested by family)

b) Annual reevaluation

Step 6. Transition plan for children turning 3

Must happen at least 90 days before but no more than 9 months prior to age 3

this information for parents, even if the schools do not coordinate the system or a child is too young to attend school. Many states have a single point of entry for early intervention information and services, which means there is a single phone number to call for everyone who lives in a state.

When parents request early intervention services, either by contacting their state's system directly or having a medical doctor or school staff member do so on their behalf, an early intervention representative asks the parents about their child's development to decide the next steps. This is called a **referral** to early intervention. Before anyone from the early intervention system can evaluate or work with their child, the parents must give their written permission. If at any time the parents are uncomfortable or unhappy with the proceedings, they may revoke their permission. The early intervention program may conduct a screening to identify children who need additional evaluation to determine whether a disability or delay exists.

IDEA outlines the rights parents have to protect both them and their child throughout the evaluation process. Each state is required to provide parents with information about their rights in an easy-to-understand format in the family's home language. IDEA regulations can be confusing for families to understand, so the law mandates that all families are entitled to a **service coordinator** to assist them in accessing the services and supports they need, including providing information about their rights.

2. Conducting an evaluation for early intervention services

A team of professionals who specialize in working with infants and toddlers evaluate the child to determine the child's current developmental functioning and the existence of a disability or delay. The members of this team—known as an **interdisciplinary team**—may evaluate the child together or individually, and the parents are an integral part of the process since they know their child best. Team members' areas of expertise vary according to the family's and/or teacher's concerns about the child. For example, if parents are concerned that their child is not speaking, a person with expertise in language development, such as a speech-language therapist, will be on the team. In addition to talking with the family—and perhaps other individuals who care for the child on a regular basis, such as child care providers or extended family members—the team members observe the child as she plays or completes tasks.

During an evaluation, the team assesses a child's functioning in five areas, or domains, of development: physical, cognitive, communication, social and emotional, and adaptive. Here are some things the team may look for in each area.

Physical development: the child's hearing, vision, and response to stimuli, as well as how he moves his arms and legs (large motor skills) and fingers and hands (small motor skills)

> **Infants:** Depending on how old the baby is, the team may look to see if he holds his head up by himself, if he is crawling, and if he can pick up small objects (toys or food).

Toddlers: The team might observe how the child walks, runs, or generally gets around. They may watch to see if she can use a fork or spoon to feed herself or manipulate small toys. They may ask if the child is very sensitive or has a very strong dislike for the taste or texture of certain foods or the feel of certain clothing or material.

Cognitive development: the way infants and toddlers learn to understand the world around them

Infants: The team may look to see if the infant recognizes a familiar caregiver or pays attention to the faces of people and visually explores her surroundings.

Toddlers: The team may look to see if the child recognizes familiar or favorite objects in his environment (such as asking "Where's the doggy?" if the child is being evaluated at home and the family dog is present). The team may also watch how the child plays with both familiar and new toys.

Communication development: the ways infants and toddlers express themselves to make their wants and needs known, as well as how well they understand what other people are saying

Infants: The team may look to see if the infant babbles and responds to his own name. With an older infant, they may watch for the child to use gestures to communicate, such as pointing to objects in the environment or shaking his head no.

Toddlers: The team may look to see if the toddler uses some words or sentences or can name familiar objects.

Social and emotional development: how the infant or toddler reacts to her own needs, the environment, and other people

Infants: The team may look to see if the infant smiles at or is easily comforted by a known caregiver. The team may also look at how the infant reacts to strangers.

Toddlers: The team may look to see if the toddler is interested in other children, imitates what other people do, and uses her parent as a safe base from which to explore her environment. The team may ask about temper tantrums and what they look like in this child if they do not observe this behavior during the assessment.

Adaptive development: the degree to which the infant or toddler assists with or completes self-help skills

Infants: The team may look to see if the infant can hold his own bottle or drink from a cup if age appropriate.

Toddlers: The team may look to see how independent the toddler is with tasks like dressing and eating by himself. The team may also ask about toilet training, bathing, and tooth brushing.

Each area of development is equally important, and although they may be evaluated separately, the areas overlap as children develop. For example, as children explore the world around them, they develop physically as well as socially and cognitively. Delays or deficits in one developmental area impact other areas.

In many states, children with specific physical or medical issues that are identified by a doctor and have a strong likelihood of leading to a delay in development are automatically eligible for early intervention services without any additional evaluations. Each state publishes a list of these conditions.

3. Determining eligibility for services

The parents and the interdisciplinary team members who evaluate the child hold an eligibility meeting to go over the results of the evaluation and decide whether the infant or toddler meets the federal and state criteria for eligibility to receive early intervention services. Other individuals may be present, such as the service coordinator and teachers or therapists who are or may be providing services. Parents are encouraged to invite other members of their family to the meeting, and they may bring an advocate to help interpret the evaluation results.

If the team determines that the child is eligible for early intervention services, they develop an **Individualized Family Service Plan** (IFSP).

4. Writing and implementing the Individualized Family Service Plan (IFSP)

Early intervention focuses on family-centered intervention processes designed to help infants and toddlers who have delays or disabilities *and* to support the whole family. The philosophy behind these services is that the family is the child's first teacher and greatest resource, so supporting the family as well as the child is critical to the child's success. For example, an infant may have low muscle tone (hypotonia) and have difficulty holding his neck up independently. If the interdisciplinary team finds the child eligible for physical therapy, a physical therapist would work with the family to find positions for breastfeeding or bottle feeding that support the child and help him develop better muscle tone. As the child gets older, the therapist might work with the family as he learns to walk independently. Early intervention services are designed as a partnership to meet families' needs and help parents and other caregivers support children's development.

Common Therapies in Early Intervention and Special Education Programs

In addition to educational services, children may require other supports and services to meet some developmental milestones. Here are some of the most common therapies young children with disabilities receive:

Physical therapy. A physical therapist (PT) provides expertise in developing large motor skills, balance, coordination, and other skills so children can move as independently as possible.

Occupational therapy. An occupational therapist (OT) provides expertise in developing small motor skills so children can become more independent in self-care routines (eating, dressing, using utensils), manipulating objects (assembling puzzles, stringing beads), using tools like scissors and pencils, and playing with peers. An OT might also work with a child who has sensory processing issues (discussed in Chapter 11).

Speech-language therapy. A speech-language therapist (SLP) provides expertise in developing speech and language skills so children can develop both expressive and receptive vocabularies to interact with peers and adults and participate in learning activities.

Intervention is planned with the family and laid out in the IFSP. The IFSP identifies appropriate services that the child and family may be eligible for, such as physical, occupational, and/or speech therapy. The service coordinator helps families arrange for and manage various service providers or agencies.

Early intervention services are provided in the **natural environment**, which refers to whatever setting the child would typically be in if she did not have a disability, such as the family's home or a child care program. In other words, the child does not have to go to a doctor's office, hospital, or school to receive services. This allows a child's family or other caregivers to learn how to integrate therapy strategies in their day-to-day routines.

Once parents consent to start implementing the IFSP, all supports and services must begin in a timely manner, usually within 30 calendar days of being agreed upon. These supports and services occur on a regular schedule based on what was agreed upon in the IFSP.

5. Reviewing the IFSP

The IFSP must be reviewed regularly to make sure that an infant or toddler is making progress and getting the services she needs. States are required under IDEA Part C to evaluate the IFSP once a year and review the document with the family every six months to make any needed changes. However, parents may request additional reviews from their service coordinator at any time.

6. Transitioning to special education at age 3

Children receive early intervention services through age 2 unless state law allows an extension of these services (Center for Parent Information and Resources 2014a). When early intervention ends, the child may transition to school-age services provided by the local public school district. The interdisciplinary team, along with the child's family, evaluates and develops an Individualized Education Program (IEP) under IDEA Part B. Transition is a process in early intervention, and it is just as much a transition *out of* early intervention as it is a transition *to* public school preschool services. Each state has different criteria for IEP eligibility under IDEA Part B than for eligibility for an

IFSP under IDEA Part C. The early intervention system takes the lead in this transition, and the service coordinator is responsible for assisting and supporting the family during this transition. The ultimate goal is a seamless transition of services between systems for the child and his family.

Special Education: Ages 3 Through 21

When children turn 3, the public school system generally takes the lead in offering supports and services for children with developmental delays and disabilities. The transition from early intervention to preschool may not be an easy one for some parents and children. They have new faces to become familiar with, and often they have built close, trusting relationships with early intervention professionals. Services may change with the transition, and the child may have a new location for services. Both the early intervention and the early childhood special education professionals must support and reassure families and children during this time.

Who pays for early intervention?
Early intervention is partly funded by federal and state monies. The federal government pays 100 percent of the cost of the evaluations, developing the IFSP, and case management. For other services like speech therapy or physical therapy, each state has its own rules about payment, including cost-shares or co-payments (Center for Parent Information and Resources 2014b).

Sequence of Identification, Assessment, and Intervention Events

Purpose	Typical Activities	Persons Involved
Child Find		
to locate and make families aware of the availability of screening	census taking, media publicity, posters, leaflets, surveys, mailings, public education programs, referrals	state personnel, school staff, volunteers, community members, health care professionals
Screening		
to identify children who may have developmental delays or disabilities	administration of screening instruments, medical exams, hearing and vision tests, completion of parent questionnaires, direct observation	teachers, physicians, other professionals, parents
Diagnostic Assessment		
to determine whether the child actually has a disability and if so, what type; to propose possible remediation strategies	formal evaluations, parent conferences, evaluation team meetings	educators, psychologists, physicians, parents, related service providers, social workers
Individualized Program Planning		
to develop an Individualized Family Service Plan (IFSP) or Individualized Education Program (IEP), program placement, and curriculum activities for the child	classroom observation, information evaluation, development of instructional objectives	teachers, parents, evaluation team personnel, other professionals

Adapted from S. Meisels & S. Atkins-Burnett, *Developmental Screening in Early Childhood: A Guide,* 5th ed. (Washington, DC: NAEYC, 2005), 7.

While IDEA covers children from birth through age 21, some of the rules and processes are different when a child begins school-age services. While the IFSP and early intervention services focus on the child and family, Part B of IDEA provides an Individualized Education Program (IEP) that focuses on the child and her educational needs.

The Special Education Referral and Evaluation Process

Each state administers its own IDEA Part B programs for children with suspected or identified disabilities. The Part B regulations outline eligibility requirements and procedures for seeking services, as well as the timelines for when the steps in the referral and evaluation processes must happen. As with the early intervention process, terminology varies from state to state and may change over time, but the basic steps are similar (see the figure below, "Individualized Education Program [IEP] Process").

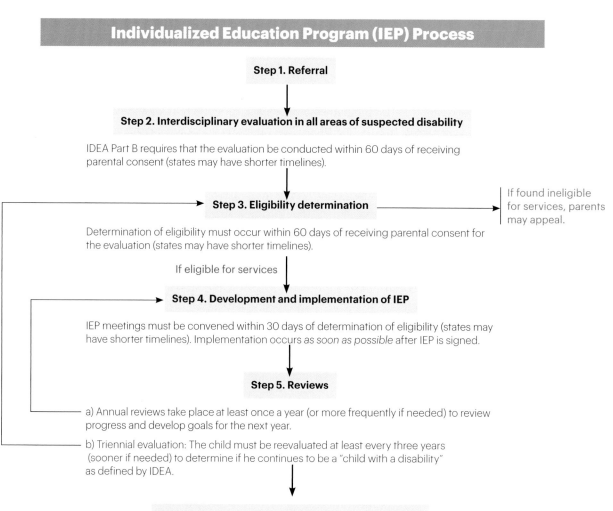

Individualized Education Program (IEP) Process

Step 1. Referral

Step 2. Interdisciplinary evaluation in all areas of suspected disability

IDEA Part B requires that the evaluation be conducted within 60 days of receiving parental consent (states may have shorter timelines).

Step 3. Eligibility determination

If found ineligible for services, parents may appeal.

Determination of eligibility must occur within 60 days of receiving parental consent for the evaluation (states may have shorter timelines).

If eligible for services

Step 4. Development and implementation of IEP

IEP meetings must be convened within 30 days of determination of eligibility (states may have shorter timelines). Implementation occurs *as soon as possible* after IEP is signed.

Step 5. Reviews

a) Annual reviews take place at least once a year (or more frequently if needed) to review progress and develop goals for the next year.

b) Triennial evaluation: The child must be reevaluated at least every three years (sooner if needed) to determine if he continues to be a "child with a disability" as defined by IDEA.

Step 6. Transition planning for postsecondary school

Planning must begin no later than ninth grade (some states may have earlier timelines). Plan is updated annually.

1. Making the referral

When an infant or toddler is receiving early intervention services, the state agency in charge of early intervention makes the referral to the local public school system when the child is about to turn 3. This is done to ensure continuity of service for the child. Service coordinators explain to families how this referral happens, what to expect, and their rights and responsibilities in this process.

For a child who has not been in an early intervention program, most of the referrals for services come from the family. When a family is concerned about their preschooler's development, they can contact their local public school and request assistance, even if the child is not yet enrolled in the school. Schools are required under **Child Find**, a system mandated by IDEA, to have policies in place to locate, identify, evaluate, and serve any child living in their communities who is suspected of having a disability and would benefit from the early intervention or special education services. As part of the Child Find process, a child may be screened to see whether she should be referred for an interdisciplinary evaluation.

Pediatricians and preschool programs can provide families with information about their state's referral and evaluation process. Referrals from families should be made in writing, highlighting their concerns and requesting that the school evaluate their child for a disability. Once the school receives this written request for an evaluation, the school must follow timelines that are outlined in the state's IDEA Part B regulations.

Other individuals, such as teachers or physicians, can also refer a child for a special education evaluation. However, no evaluation can occur without parental consent.

2. Conducting the evaluation

Evaluations to determine if the child has a disability are individualized and based on the child's needs and the family's concerns. The evaluation process must use valid, reliable assessments and assess all areas of suspected disability. As in the early intervention system, evaluations are completed by an interdisciplinary team of experts. The results of the evaluation are then used to determine if the child meets the state's eligibility requirements for special education services.

3. Determining eligibility for services

The team that conducts the evaluation interprets the results to decide if the child meets the federal and state criteria to receive special education services. If the child is eligible, then the team and family work together to develop a program for the child. Should the team decide, based on evaluations, that the child does not have a disability and is not eligible to receive services, the process ends. If parents disagree with this decision, they have the right under IDEA to challenge it.

Disability Categories Under IDEA

The primary goal of IDEA is to ensure that special education and related services are available to children with disabilities in public schools. While each state sets its own eligibility criteria for these services, IDEA defines some specific disabilities that states use to help make their own definitions. Those disabilities identified in IDEA are

- Learning disability
- Intellectual disability (originally termed mental retardation in the law, but changed with the enactment of Rosa's Law of 2011 [Public Law 111-256])
- Autism (now known under the broader term of autism spectrum disorder)
- Hearing impairment
- Visual impairment
- Orthopedic impairment (may be called physical disability)
- Other health impairment (such as attention-deficit/hyperactivity disorder, diabetes, asthma, epilepsy)
- Multiple disabilities
- Speech or language impairment
- Emotional disturbance (may be called behavior disorder or emotional disability)
- Deafness
- Deaf-blindness
- Traumatic brain injury

Developmental delay, a nonspecific category, may be used for children between the ages of 3 and 9 if they have delays in one or more areas of development.

Children are considered to have a disability if, after proper assessment, they meet the criteria for one of these disabilities *and* require special education or related services due to the disability (Center for Parent Information and Resources 2014a). Simply having a disability is not usually enough to be eligible; the disability must also affect the child's educational performance. This does not mean that a child with a disability has to be failing in school to be eligible to receive services but that the disability impacts the child's ability to learn.

4. Writing the Individualized Education Program (IEP)

Once a child is found eligible for services, an **Individualized Education Program** (IEP) is written by a team of people, including the parents, teacher(s), and some members of the evaluation team. The IEP specifies the following:

» The child's Present Level of Academic Achievement and Functional Performance (PLAAFP), a description of the child's current functioning in school or at home

» Individualized goals to be addressed in the following year

» Supports and services needed to access education, participate in instruction, and make progress toward the program's standards and the IEP goals

The location where services will take place is also noted in the IEP. Placement must be in the **least restrictive environment** (LRE) for that child, meaning that to the maximum extent possible, the child is educated with his same-age peers who do not have disabilities. For many preschoolers with disabilities, this might mean they attend public school preschools, Head Start programs, or private preschool or child care programs. The LRE varies from child to child and may change over time. The IEP team may decide that a child with a disability will be best served in a classroom that is specifically designed to educate only students with disabilities, or that the best solution may be more than one placement, with part of the day spent in a classroom designed only for students with disabilities and the other part included in a classroom with their peers who do not have disabilities.

Although the decision is always individualized for each child, the goal is to provide children with as much access to programs with their peers as possible. Many professionals and families use the terms **inclusion**, *full inclusion*, or *inclusion class* to describe settings in which children with disabilities are educated alongside their same-age peers. IDEA uses the terms *natural environment* and *least restrictive environment* to describe the preferred settings for educating children with disabilities.

Once the IEP is written, families must give consent before it can take effect. In most states, to demonstrate this consent parents are required to sign a document stating that they are in agreement with what is written in the IEP and they want the IEP to be implemented. Parents should review the final copy of the IEP before they sign. If at any time the parents feel that a change in the IEP is warranted, they may request a new IEP meeting.

5. Reviewing the IEP

The IEP team meets at least once a year to review a child's IEP and identify the progress he is making toward his current goals. They also develop new IEP goals for the following year as well as decide what supports and services will be offered. Parents or school personnel can request additional meetings or amendments to the IEP if the child is not making progress toward his goals, or if the child is progressing better than expected and the goals must be adjusted to reflect this.

6. Transition planning for postsecondary school

When the student is 16 years old, the IEP team, including the student and family, develops goals that will help prepare the student for adult life, including the skills needed to have a job, live independently, and be a productive member of society.

Partnering with Families Through the IFSP and IEP Processes

When Mrs. Lopez takes her just-turned-2 son, Sebastian, to his pediatrician, she mentions that both she and Sebastian's child care teacher have noticed that Sebastian shows no interest in playing with or talking to other children. In fact, he shows little interest in other people at all and uses only a few words to communicate. He plays with cars by himself for long stretches of time, lining them all up in a row. Even when Mariana, his teacher, prompts Sebastian to play alongside another child, he continues to focus all his attention on his own play. During group times he sometimes participates in music activities, but otherwise he sits off by himself and looks away from the group. Mariana has suggested that Sebastian's mother talk to his doctor.

Inclusion is the practice of teaching young children with disabilities in the same classrooms with children their own age who do not have disabilities. While you may occasionally hear the older term *mainstreaming* to mean inclusion, the two are not interchangeable. Mainstreaming describes a child with a disability participating in a general education class for just part of the day or for specific activities.

The IEP is *not* the curriculum Many IEPs contain goals related to specific deficits and isolated skills a child needs to acquire. Unfortunately, these goals often become the de facto curriculum for the child. Keep in mind that a child's IEP is intended as an *addition* to your program's curriculum and standards. Use it as a tool to help you implement, not replace, the curriculum you use with all children.

Dr. Jimenez, the pediatrician, asks Mrs. Lopez several questions and decides to use the M-CHAT-R/F screening tool with Sebastian and Mrs. Lopez to get a better picture of what might be going on with Sebastian. The checklist indicates that he is at high risk for autism spectrum disorder. Dr. Jimenez feels that Sebastian might benefit from additional education options and suggests that Mrs. Lopez and her husband contact the early intervention program for an evaluation. After thinking about this, they decide to call.

Jill, the family's new service coordinator, and a small team of professionals come to the Lopez house to play with Sebastian, evaluate his needs, talk to his parents, and answer their questions. Sebastian does not talk much while they are there, but he explores some of the toys they have brought. Mr. Lopez asks if the team is able to tell if his son has autism spectrum disorder. While the team members say they cannot diagnose Sebastian, they can share their findings with Dr. Jimenez so she can make a better determination about a diagnosis as he gets older.

At a meeting with Mr. and Mrs. Lopez to discuss the evaluation results, everyone agrees that Sebastian is eligible for early intervention services due to a delay in his ability to communicate as well as a delay in social and emotional development. They decide that he may benefit from speech therapy the most to help him learn to interact and communicate with others. Mariana and Rob, the speech therapist, meet with Mr. and Mrs. Lopez and Jill to develop an IFSP for Sebastian and outline the goals they will work on with him and his parents. Rob will come to the center twice a week to work on these goals in class, and Mrs. Lopez and Mariana will work together to carry over these goals at home and when Rob is not at the center.

For several months Rob works on getting Sebastian to play and interact with a few of the other children who crowd around Rob when he comes. Slowly Sebastian responds, and later Mariana notices that he has started to play alongside his classmates even when Rob isn't there. Mr. and Mrs. Lopez are pleased with this progress, as is Mariana. Mariana decides to ask Rob for other strategies she can use in the classroom to build on Sebastian's progress.

Parents and teachers can be strong partners in making sure that every child receives what she needs to be successful. NAEYC's *Code of Ethical Conduct and Statement of Commitment* reminds early childhood educators that it is their ethical responsibility to children "to advocate for and ensure that all children, including those with special needs, have access to the support services needed to be successful" (2016, 2). You may be the first professional to recognize that a child has a delay in development or a disability, and you have a professional responsibility to discuss your concerns with the child's family as soon as possible. Many parents rely on teachers for professional advice, and you need to be prepared to share your observations along with information the family can use to seek additional help if they wish. Advocating for children and becoming partners with parents is an essential role for every teacher, as is supporting families as they advocate for their own children.

Families and early childhood educators look at children through different lenses. Families see the child primarily at home in the context of everyday life with individuals he is very familiar with, and educators see the child primarily in programs in the context of early learning, alongside other children near the same age. Different environments, with different expectations for a child—no wonder parents and educators sometimes see children differently! Regularly communicating with a family about their child—his ups and downs, what he likes and doesn't, how he interacts with others—gives everyone a better understanding of the child's strengths and needs. It also assures the family that you care about their child and know him very well, and it helps to build their trust in you. Trust opens the door to being able to share your concerns with them.

Understanding Emotions

Discussing your concerns about a child's development with a family is never easy, but it is important to help the child and family be able to access any supports or services they may be entitled to that will help the child be successful. When you share your concerns about a child, parents may have different reactions than you expect, including dismissing your observations or becoming angry, and they might need time to process this information and their feelings before moving forward (Ray, Pewitt-Kinder, & George 2009). Accept this, and avoid making judgmental statements. Make the effort to carefully listen to what they are saying, and encourage them to talk about their own concerns, doubts, and worries so you can understand their perspective.

Also, emphasize the child's positive traits. Every child has strengths, and it is important to talk about what a child *can* do and not just focus on what she *can't* do.

Being Prepared

Keep written documentation of your concerns about a child's development, or the family's concerns they share with you, in different situations and when different demands are put on the child. Having this information makes it easier for you, the family, and the child's doctor to note patterns in the child's development and see if he's making progress. The information you provide may help the doctor diagnose a delay or a disability, and in turn, this diagnosis can help determine if the child is eligible for early intervention or special education services.

Tips for Communicating Your Concerns to Parents

Here are some things to consider as you prepare to talk with a child's family:

» **Understand the importance of time and place.** Plan to talk with the family in person, making sure that all of you can set aside ample time for this conversation and that you have privacy. Do not try to have this conversation at drop-off or pickup time when families are in a rush, or during scheduled conferences when there is a narrow window of time and other parents are waiting for their meetings. Arrange a space to discuss the issues in private, without other adults or children being able to overhear or interrupt.

» **Start with the positives.** Every child has positive qualities—highlight them at the start of the conversation. Let the parent know what their child does well and encourage them to talk about what they see as their child's strengths.

» **Remember that words matter.** Choose your words carefully, and avoid stating what you think *may* be wrong or your opinions about what the next steps should be. Discuss only what you actually observe and document in the classroom. Talk *with* the parents, not just to them. Let them ask as many questions as they need. And listen well.

» **Offer additional information and support.** Be prepared to help the parents with the next step in getting help for their child. Have information and resources available at the meeting so you can discuss them if the parents ask. Be respectful of the parents. Offer to help, but if the parents decline assistance at this time, do not force the issue. They may be ready to ask for help later, and then you can give it.

» **Trust your instincts.** While it is difficult to tell parents that their child may have a delay or disability, your professional instincts and experiences are a valuable resource. Trust them.

Despite their experience and expertise in the area of early childhood development, teachers need to be respectful of the family and their wishes, as well as careful not to share their opinions or unsolicited advice. Having concrete information about how their child is functioning in the classroom is essential for families to make a decision and seek more information about a potential delay or disability.

3

Where to Start: Developmentally Appropriate Practice, Inclusion, and Universal Design

The number of children with identified disabilities included in general education classrooms and programs alongside their peers without disabilities increases every year. While having a child with a disability included in their class may seem overwhelming for teachers with little or no training in special education, the first thing all teachers need to know is that they are not alone. Teaching a young child with a disability involves the support of many different people who are there not only for the child and family but also to provide the teacher with the resources she or he needs to be effective. The more you understand how to effectively teach a child with a disability in an infant, toddler, or preschool program, or in a general education elementary classroom, the more successful the child will be.

So how do you meet the needs of a group of children with widely varying abilities, strengths, and needs? Where do you start? Building on the idea that good practice for children with disabilities is good practice for *all* children, you start with developmentally appropriate practice. Together with universal design, discussed later in this chapter, developmentally appropriate practice lays the foundation for successful inclusion in early childhood programs.

Developmentally Appropriate Practice

You're probably keenly aware that while the children in your classroom may all be similar ages, they are not all at the same developmental level. Early childhood is a time of rapid change for most children, and they grow, develop new skills, and acquire new knowledge right before your eyes. Each child comes to your program having many different experiences as well as unique strengths and challenges. You need to be perceptive and flexible to support each child's learning and development.

Because of children's varied needs, when planning for *all* students, effective early childhood teachers remain true to the guidelines of their profession referred to as **developmentally**

appropriate practice (DAP). DAP is an approach to teaching based on research on how young children develop and learn and on what is known about effective early education. It is designed to promote young children's optimal learning and development.

In its position statement on developmentally appropriate practice, the National Association for the Education of Young Children (NAEYC) (2009) outlines research on the principles of child development and how young children learn to help teachers intentionally plan routines and activities that promote the success of every child, including children with developmental delays or identified disabilities. Developmentally appropriate practice

» Requires both meeting children where they are—which means that teachers must get to know them well—and enabling them to reach goals that are both challenging and achievable

» Is appropriate to children's age and developmental status, attuned to them as unique individuals, and responsive to the social and cultural contexts in which they live

» Does not mean making things easier for children but ensuring that goals and experiences are suited to their learning and development and challenging enough to promote their progress and interest

» Is based on knowledge—not on assumptions—from research on how children learn and develop (Copple & Bredekamp 2009)

Core Considerations of DAP and Children with Disabilities

The NAEYC position statement on DAP (2009) highlights three core considerations for identifying developmentally appropriate practices in early childhood classrooms. These considerations, identified below, apply to working with all children. They do not matter less when children with delays or disabilities are included in the classroom.

1. **Knowing about child development and early learning.** Understanding child development and what is and is not expected of children at specific ages is helpful when making broad decisions about the classroom. While some children are further behind developmentally than their peers, understanding *how* children learn at different stages of development (for example, through play and exploring materials) is helpful for designing classroom routines and activities that are broad and flexible enough for children at many different developmental levels to participate and be successful.

2. **Knowing what is individually appropriate.** Every child has different strengths and needs, and these vary over time and in different situations. Understanding each child as an individual is a key factor for teaching children with delays or disabilities. Working from a position of strength and what a child *can* do, instead of focusing on her deficits, helps you adapt and modify routines and activities so the child can participate as independently as possible.

3. **Knowing what is culturally important.** Looking at the child as a member of a larger community and understanding his family's cultural background and values—especially his home language—are essential when you plan classroom routines and activities and when you interact with his family.

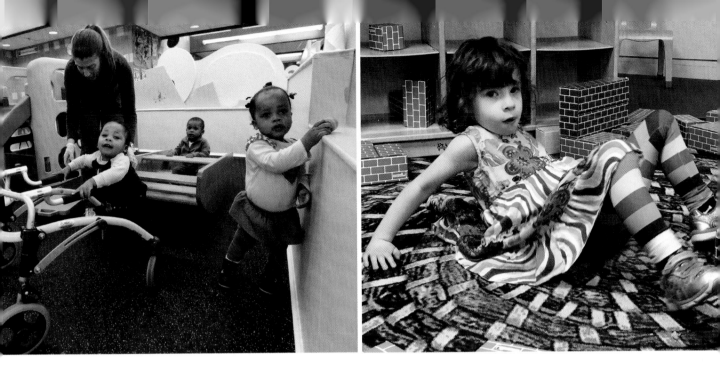

The principles and considerations of DAP, along with research-based evidence about curriculum and teaching effectiveness, form a solid basis for decision making in early childhood inclusive classrooms.

Inclusion as a Philosophy and a Practice

Inclusion is part of a philosophy that everyone is more alike than different, that differences make classrooms and experiences richer, that everyone—children with and without disabilities, families, and education professionals—benefits when children are educated together, and that no one should be segregated because they are different in some way.

Successful inclusion offers numerous benefits for everyone. Through everyday classroom interactions with their peers, children with disabilities learn social skills, gain a sense of confidence and independence, and exhibit more appropriate behavior. Their peers often become more understanding and willing to help others. Children feel a sense of belonging. According to the US Departments of Health and Human Services and Education (HHS & ED 2015),

» Being meaningfully included as a member of society is the first step to equal opportunity, one of America's most cherished ideals, and is every person's right—a right supported by our laws.

» Research indicates that meaningful inclusion is beneficial to children with and without disabilities.

» Preliminary research shows that operating inclusive early childhood programs is not necessarily more expensive than operating separate early childhood programs for children with disabilities.

» Meaningful inclusion can support children with disabilities in reaching their full potential, resulting in broad societal benefits. (2)

Research and experience confirm that many, if not most, children with disabilities can be successfully included in high-quality early childhood programs (Green, Terry, & Gallagher 2014; HHS & ED 2015; Strain & Bovey 2011). Achieving this requires collaboration among all professionals and families, examining your own beliefs, knowing where and how to access resources, and having strong administrative support.

Inclusion looks different for each child—it always depends on what a particular child needs to be successful. Many children have difficulty with some routines and activities during the classroom day, but not with all of them. You might change or modify a specific routine or activity a child has trouble with so it is not as difficult for her, or you might set different expectations for that child for that activity only; most likely, this would not be necessary for every part of the school day.

Depending on a child's needs, he might participate in a classroom with his peers without disabilities for part of the day rather than full time. Sadly, many children do not have even this opportunity; in schools and programs across the country, large numbers of children with disabilities are still served in segregated special education programs with little chance to participate in high-quality programs designed for all children (HHS & ED 2015). Teachers, families, and others must continue to advocate for change and more resources and work to find opportunities for children to engage in programs and activities with their peers.

Barriers to Including Young Children with Disabilities

There are legitimate challenges and barriers that states, programs, and families face when promoting and providing inclusive opportunities for children with disabilities. The joint policy statement on inclusion from the US Departments of Heath and Human Services and Education identifies several challenges to inclusive programming for young children:

» **Attitudes and beliefs of parents and educators.** Many programs report significant misinformation among families and educators about the benefits and practicality of inclusive programs in schools and communities. Many people worry that including children strains the classroom teacher's resources, resulting in the needs of both the children with disabilities and the children without disabilities going unmet. While this challenge can be overcome in programs with strong collaboration among teachers and specialists and support from administrators, when these are lacking it is a very real concern.

» **Lack of expertise of the early childhood workforce.** Many early childhood educators believe they lack knowledge about individualized instruction, child development, and early childhood pedagogy that is needed to effectively educate children with disabilities alongside their peers.

» **Lack of comprehensive services.** Children with disabilities frequently receive related, specially designed instruction from professionals in speech-language therapy, physical therapy, and occupational therapy. However, expertise in these areas may not be available in private child care programs in the community, and bringing in outside resources can be costly. When such resources *are* available, too often teachers are not shown how to implement therapy practices in their daily routines with children.

» **Limited time and commitment to build partnerships.** Therapists and special education teachers or early intervention providers often lack the time to collaborate with each other, or with classroom teachers and families, on the goals they are working on with the child and to share the progress or challenges they are seeing. This lack of time and commitment to coordinate services inhibits the development of the strong relationships among the professionals who help make inclusive programs more successful (HHS & ED 2015).

Universal Design

To effectively support the needs of all children in your classroom or program, think about ways to design the classroom space, routines, and activities so they are adaptable and can be used with and by many children in a variety of ways. With flexibility built into the design from the start, all children can access the curriculum, process information in a way that works for them, and demonstrate what they know (Conn-Powers et al. 2006). With a continued focus on developmentally appropriate practices and your school's or program's learning standards, this proactive approach supports children's strengths and balances the needs of all children. It is the most efficient and effective way to develop inclusive classrooms and programs.

This concept of proactive design and flexibility, known as **universal design** (UD), was first applied to architecture. For example, when new buildings are designed, ramps are built in place of, or in addition to, stairs, allowing anyone to enter and travel throughout the buildings. Some people are able to use stairs, but a ramp is flexible enough for anyone to use. Similarly,

DEC's Recommended Practices

The *DEC Recommended Practices* (2014) provides guidelines for early childhood and special education professionals and families to promote the development of children with delays or disabilities from birth through age 5. The practices "support children's access and participation in inclusive settings and natural environments and address cultural, linguistic, and ability diversity" (3). The document addresses eight areas:

- Leadership
- Assessment
- Environment
- Family
- Instruction
- Interaction
- Teaming and Collaboration
- Transition

Universal design (UD) refers to designing materials, products, and environments to be used by the greatest number of people without the need to adapt or change them (The Center for Universal Design 1997). The principles of UD are discussed on pages 28–29.

Universal design for learning (UDL) is the application of UD principles to education to proactively design curriculum and classroom practices so the greatest number of students can benefit without the need for adaptations or changes (Rose & Meyer 2006). The principles of UDL include

- Multiple means of **representation**— offering students a range of ways to obtain information and knowledge
- Multiple means of **expression**— giving students different ways to demonstrate what they know
- Multiple means of **engagement**— providing a variety of ways to challenge and motivate students to participate and learn (CAST 2011)

automatic doors that open by themselves when a person approaches a store or other building make entry and exit more flexible, which in turn enables more people to use it—and not just those with disabilities. A person pushing a child in a stroller or pulling luggage may find it easier to use ramps and automatic doors, too. Applying this process of UD proactively results in environments that can be used by everyone in a similar manner.

The concept of UD is also applied in the context of teaching and learning. In the early 1990s the Center for Applied Special Technology (CAST) began promoting the concept of **universal design for learning** (UDL) as a way to design curriculum to include many options for accessing clear goals, flexible materials and methods, and embedded assessment to support the needs of many different learners (Rose & Meyer 2006).

While the principles of UDL have piqued the interest of many early childhood teachers and school leaders, current evidence-based classroom practices using the principles of UDL frequently focus on the needs of children in upper elementary, high school, and college classes to access materials such as textbooks and online learning opportunities (Meyer, Rose, & Gordon 2014). While some UDL practices may not be as applicable to classrooms and programs that serve young children, the bigger concept of universal design can be used to increase access and success for children of all ages.

Using the principles of universal design in early childhood classrooms and programs as a framework to design learning environments, routines, and activities to make them as flexible and responsive as possible provides supports for all children and reduces the barriers for children with disabilities. Just as ramps and automatic doors help people without disabilities, UD practices can help children who do not have disabilities, including those who speak a home language other than English or who have developmental delays but not disabilities. UD practices are also useful to consider in your collaboration with families. Provide multiple means for sharing program and child information with families, different opportunities for them to support their child at home and in the program, and many ways for them to be involved.

When designing or redesigning your classroom or program spaces and activities, consider the seven principles of universal design through the lens of developmentally appropriate practices (The Center for Universal Design 1997).

1. **Equitable use:** All children use the same materials and spaces, which avoids segregating or calling undue attention to a child with a disability. Instead of an easel for a child who uses a wheelchair and an art table for everyone else, easels are set up for everyone to use. The entire curriculum engages children with diverse abilities.

2. **Flexible use:** Children use the same materials and curriculum as everyone else but in varied ways or with adaptations to accommodate a disability or personal preference. Switches added to cause-and-effect toys make them more manageable to activate. Books with paper clips attached to the pages enable a child to turn the pages more easily. Children learn concepts and practice skills at their own pace.

3. **Simple and intuitive:** The design of the spaces and materials is easy for everyone to understand. Every material has a specific place and is labeled in different ways, making finding and cleaning up materials easy to understand and accomplish.

4. **Perceptible information:** The spaces and materials provide information to children in a number of ways. Pictures, words (in English and children's home languages), and braille are used together to bring meaning to children with language delays or vision impairments and to dual language learners (children learning English while continuing to develop their home language). Beginning braille signage is posted around the classroom for children who have vision impairments and will be braille readers. Lights flicker when the fire alarm goes off so children with hearing impairments understand the same information as everyone else in the classroom.

5. **Tolerance for error:** Teachers design learning environments and materials that provide ongoing assistance and accommodate children when they don't get things correct the first time. The design eliminates or minimizes hazards and limits the frustration some children feel when they make mistakes. Some wooden blocks can have felt attached to one side, making them less likely to fall over if a child inadvertently knocks into them while building. The settings on classroom touchscreen computers or communication boards can be adjusted so that they do not react to an unintended touch. Software or apps have an undo button so children can go back. Older children can work with easy-to-write-with markers and erasable whiteboards for some tasks typically done with paper and pencil.

6. **Low physical effort:** Spaces and materials are set up so they are easier to use by all children. Automatic soap and paper towel dispensers in the bathroom, along with a sink that turns on and off when children place their hands under the faucet, reduce the physical effort needed by children with low strength or who use a wheelchair. Instructional materials are accessible, and the schedule allows for varying energy levels.

7. **Size and space for approach and use:** Spaces in the classroom allow everyone physical access and encourage learning. There are chairs for children who use wheelchairs to sit at the table so they are at the same eye level as their classmates. Outdoor areas have ramps and are accessible in other ways to children with physical needs. There are spaces for small and large group activities and lessons, places for one or two children to work together, and quiet retreat areas.

"Universal Design in the Classroom Checklist" on pages 30–31 offers helpful questions to consider about UD and ways to incorporate its practices in your own setting.

Universal Design in the Classroom Checklist

Classroom Practices	Does/is my classroom . . .	What can I do to incorporate this practice?
Physical environment	Accessible for all children?	Make sure children can use each part of the classroom in a similar way. If everyone sits on the carpet for group time or a class meeting, provide a way for a child with a disability to do so without needing an adult to hold or support her.
		Work with a physical therapist to design accessible spaces for children with physical disabilities. Work with other professionals to design spaces if the child has other sensory needs.
		Find ways to absorb background noise that can distract children as they are learning.
	Include equipment and materials that are easy to use by everyone?	Provide ways for children to access all of the materials in the room as independently as possible.
		Identify containers of materials to help a child with a visual impairment recognize what is inside.
		Color-code materials so they are easy for children with learning disabilities to match up. For example, cover math workbooks in the same color as children's math homework folders.
		Provide dress-up items with multiple ways to fasten them.
		Have a child keep books and other materials on a shelf next to her desk instead of inside a dark desk so the materials are easier to find.
	Designed with safety in mind?	Develop plans and procedures with families and other members of the interdisciplinary team for fires or other classroom emergencies.
		Develop materials, like class-made books, that help children learn what to expect during a safety drill.
		Keep pathways clear and free of tripping hazards for a child who uses a mobility device or has a visual impairment.
Class climate	Welcome everyone, including children who spend part of the day or week in the classroom?	Treat every child as a member of the class, even if he is not in the room full time. Work with the child's other teachers and team members to make educational decisions together.
		Display every child's work and creations in the classroom. Include everyone in group photos of the class, and put each child's name on every class list (especially the ones that go home) so children and families know that the child is a member of your classroom, even if it is only occasionally.
		Provide elementary-age children with their own space in the classroom (a desk and chair, if that is what the other children use) so they feel included during whole group and small group instruction.
	Avoid stereotyping?	Do not assume that a child with a disability needs assistance with a particular activity or routine. Always give the child time to try to accomplish the task as independently as possible.
	Avoid segregating or stigmatizing any student?	Encourage other adults in the classroom to not draw unnecessary or unwarranted attention to a child with a disability. Avoid having an adult always by the child's side.
		Support a peer buddy program so children have same-age peers to play with during less-structured time, like in the cafeteria and on the playground.

Classroom Practices	Does/is my classroom . . .	What can I do to incorporate this practice?
Interactions	Enable effective teacher–child communication?	Speak directly to the child with a disability the same way you speak to other children. Give him enough wait time to process what you are saying. Model what you *intend* to model for the child's peers who do not have disabilities. Actions speak louder than words, so make sure you are communicating the messages you want them to receive about how to interact with the child with a disability.
	Have multiple ways for children to communicate with each other?	Provide ways for a child who uses little or no speech to communicate with other children without adult assistance. Teach all of the children in the classroom to use the child's preferred method of communication—picture symbols, sign language, and so on—and model it with everyone.
	Encourage cooperative work?	Design activities that require more than one child's participation to accomplish the task. Assign peer buddies, instead of an adult, to assist children with disabilities. Scaffold group work for older students so everyone knows what they are expected to contribute. Remind all children that everyone can contribute something to every activity.

Is Including a Child Enough? Ensuring Access, Participation, and Progress

Together, developmentally appropriate practices, inclusion, and universal design offer a powerful foundation for meeting the needs of children with disabilities. The 1997 amendments to IDEA stipulate, however, that children with disabilities are entitled to **access**, **participation**, and **progress** within the general education curriculum (Hitchcock et al. 2002). These three elements, which often require individualized modifications and supports for children, are key to truly providing children the educational environment they need to develop to their full potential, and they deserve close consideration.

Access

Access refers to the policies put in place to make sure that every student has an equal opportunity to take full advantage of an education. There are different types of access.

Physical access. It may seem basic, but this kind of access is indispensable to a child with a physical disability, so look at ways the child can enter the building and navigate the classroom and whether the widths of the classroom and bathroom doors accommodate a child using a mobility device. Classroom arrangement and physical access to materials also impact a child's access to education. Is there enough space for the child to access all of the centers? Can he sit with the other children during whole group time? Can a child with a physical disability or visual impairment reach all play and instructional materials and open containers, boxes, or drawers where materials are stored?

Social and emotional access. Inclusion provides children with access to one of the most essential elements for development: a diverse group of peers and adults with whom to form relationships and friendships and learn social interactions. Participating with peers gives children opportunities to learn and practice sharing, taking turns, resolving conflicts, and exchanging and building on each other's ideas. These skills benefit them not only in the present but also in later schooling and community and work life.

Access and the ADA

The Americans with Disabilities Act (ADA) requires that all "places of public accommodation," including child care centers and schools, make reasonable modifications when necessary to accommodate individual needs (Child Care Law Center 2011). These might include adding ramps, changing doorknobs, or lowering water fountains. Such changes cannot impose an "undue hardship," meaning they would be difficult to complete or would incur a significant expense (Child Care Law Center 2011).

Access to a high-quality curriculum used by all learners. The general education curriculum is the overall plan that guides the content, expectations, and outcomes for a school or program. A program with a high-quality curriculum sets high, developmentally appropriate expectations for every child and establishes routines, activities, and supports. One of the most vital aspects of access to an inclusive classroom with a high-quality curriculum is the ongoing opportunity for children to interact with peers who are at varying developmental and academic levels. Inclusive classrooms typically have higher expectations for students with disabilities and provide daily opportunities for them to be challenged (Gupta, Henninger, & Vinh 2014). Children in such programs demonstrate stronger cognitive gains than children who are not included in programs where a high-quality early childhood curriculum is implemented (Peters 2004; Strain & Bovey 2011).

Participation

Participation in education goes beyond having access to educational opportunities and being physically included in the classroom. Participation means to be engaged—to be part of the group and of the learning.

Physical participation. Participation goes hand in hand with independence. Giving children ways to be independent within the routines and activities of the day limits the amount of time they are dependent on adults, stretches children's skills and problem solving, and enables children to participate more naturally.

You can adapt certain classroom materials to make it easier for some children to participate without changing the material too drastically for everyone else. For example, if a child has difficulty with hand-eye coordination or lacks strength to snap or button up dress-up clothes, add Velcro fasteners to the clothes. Put no-slip material under a child's plate at snack time or under his art or work items. Some children with sensory needs focus better during group activities if they have a heavy blanket or small bean bag on their laps.

Look for ways to adapt routines, too. Transitions to snack or lunch time can be hectic, and some children may take longer to complete this transition. Playing a game like musical chairs during the transition can help; with control over the pacing, you can have one child at a time transition to washing her hands and going to the snack table. An activity like this keeps other children engaged while giving some children the extra time they need to be independent.

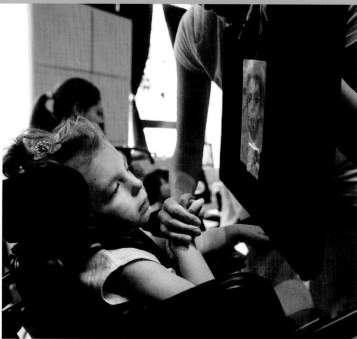

Language/communication participation. The ability to understand and use language to communicate with adults and peers opens both social and academic opportunities. Enhance participation by children who have communication issues by teaching and using both unaided and aided communication strategies. **Unaided communication** uses parts of a child's body, including gestures, facial expressions, and hands (sign language), to communicate (Eisenberg 2015). Use simple sign language throughout the day even if no one in the class has a hearing loss; this adds another way for some students to understand or be understood. **Aided communication** is the use of objects, pictures, photos, or specific devices to communicate (Eisenberg 2015). Provide simple pictures that express words and feelings to help students communicate with adults or each other. Such devices that help children communicate are called **augmentative and alternative communication** (AAC) devices.

The best way for everyone to participate in the classroom is to provide several means of communicating. Remind all children that no one communicates using only speech, and demonstrate how people use simple gestures or facial expressions to understand what others are trying to say.

At times, you need to explicitly teach children with disabilities how to interact appropriately with others. Break down social (or academic) skills into smaller, more manageable parts and teach them one at a time. Children's peers can also help teach and reinforce these new skills. When you are consistent and have peers model what's expected, children are less likely to experience frustration and isolation and are more likely to be accepted by others (Gupta, Henninger, & Vinh 2014).

Schedules. While therapies are extremely important for helping a child develop skills, removing a child from the classroom to receive therapy in a separate setting inhibits participation with peers and removes the child from the routines of the day. Embedding these interventions (discussed in more detail in Chapter 4) in the daily routines of the classroom can help increase participation in classroom activities and is often more effective for helping the child learn to use the skills in more situations.

Progress

Progress in the context of early childhood education refers to a child's growth and development over time. Learning is not linear, and because there are surges and plateaus of development along the way, assessing a young child's progress is a complex task.

Whether you are assessing a child's knowledge and skills she's gained with regard to your program's learning standards or her progress toward her IFSP or IEP goals, the most effective and reliable way to do so is to embed assessments into daily routines and activities. When you assess a child within the natural setting and routines, the assessment should not look or feel any different than activities or interactions the child normally engages in during the day (Washington State OSPI 2008).

Monitoring a child's progress toward the early learning standards. Most states have adopted statewide early learning standards that provide a general framework for what children should know and be able to do at specific ages. These standards apply to all children in the state, including those with disabilities. Some children with disabilities may have difficulty reaching the age or grade goals identified in the standards, but they should make measurable progress toward them.

To truly gauge whether a child has made progress, collect multiple sources of evidence over time. Many formal assessment systems—including Teaching Strategies GOLD, The Work Sampling System (WSS), and the HighScope Child Observation Record (COR)—guide teachers on what kind of evidence to collect, how many sources of evidence are needed, and how often to collect the evidence. Together, these pieces become a portfolio reflecting the knowledge and skills a student has gained over time.

Monitoring a child's progress toward IFSP and IEP goals. Children with disabilities also have individualized goals stated in their IFSP or IEP, and educators must ensure that children are making measurable progress toward these goals. IFSP and IEP goals do not replace the state standards; they add more specific information about what the child needs to work on and how to measure his progress. IFSP and IEP goals are written in a specific format so they are observable and measurable, and they outline specific criteria that indicate how often data must be collected for each goal and what it looks like when a child has mastered a goal. (See the charts on pages 45–48 in Chapter 4 for examples.)

....

With your knowledge of developmentally appropriate practice, you can proactively design your classroom and curriculum to provide all children with access, participation, and opportunities to make progress. As you think about the environment, the schedule, and the interactions children have with you and with each other, ask yourself, "What else can I do to make sure a child with a disability is successful in my classroom?"

4 Individualizing Supports and Interventions

Christopher is excited to start as a first grade teacher at his new school. His class will include five students with disabilities, but even though Christopher has no background in special education, he isn't worried. There will be plenty of help from Ming-Na, the special education teacher, and several therapists, including Kieran, the occupational therapist. Each of them will work with some or all of the students with disabilities in his class. A few weeks before school starts, Christopher receives copies of each student's IEP. Some parts are confusing to him, and he sets them aside to review them in more detail with Ming-Na.

Christopher also receives the teacher editions of the textbooks he is required to use. For math, each day the lesson starts with an animated video introducing a math concept. Christopher thinks these videos are too childish for first graders and wants to teach the concepts himself. When he brings this up with the principal, Anita, she advises him to show the videos *and* teach the concept himself while he gets to know his class and figure out how the students learn best. She reminds him that presenting the lessons a few different ways gives everyone a chance to learn.

Ming-Na is assigned to co-teach with Christopher most of the day. She previously taught his five students with disabilities last year and is familiar with how they learn best and how their individual impairments impact them in the classroom. While she looks forward to co-teaching some subjects, like science and social studies, she isn't sure it will work well for other subjects, especially math and language arts. Ming-Na had planned to take the five students with disabilities to a quiet corner of the classroom so she could teach them math and language arts, but Christopher wants to split the class into two groups based on how the children learn best and alternate teaching each group. This way, both teachers will have the chance to work with every child for math and language arts.

Ming-Na doesn't want to disagree with Christopher since she feels this is his classroom, but his idea makes her uncomfortable for several reasons. She feels that the children with disabilities will not get the support they need if they are included in a bigger group. Splitting the class in half also means that she would be teaching a much larger group than she is used to, and she would be teaching students without disabilities for the first time.

She finally voices her concerns in a meeting with Anita and Christopher. Christopher is surprised and bothered that Ming-Na feels that this is *his* class; he intended for her to feel like it is *their* class. After listening to her concerns, he and Ming-Na discuss their ideas further and write up a plan they both feel will be effective.

Kieran, the occupational therapist, works with one student in the class, Juan. Due to cerebral palsy, Juan has trouble with small motor control, especially writing and dressing himself. Christopher and Ming-Na are both concerned that Juan misses math twice a week so he can work with Kieran in a separate room. Kieran agrees that this is not ideal, but the agency he works for and Juan's IEP determine the schedule and process.

Christopher, Ming-Na, and Kieran decide to get input from the IEP team and Juan's family. Based on these conversations, they revise Juan's IEP so that Kieran will spend one day a week with Juan in math class to help him to use some new materials, like a slant board and a no-slip surface on his desk. On another day, Kieran will meet with Christopher and Ming-Na before school to discuss any issues Juan might have and what they can do.

Christopher, Ming-Na, and Kieran watch for any regression of Juan's skills once this new IEP is put into place. Kieran is happy to report that Juan continues to make progress toward his goals, and Christopher and Ming-Na are delighted to see that Juan's handwriting is improving.

Teachers are tasked with developing strategies to support all of the learners in their classroom. Although using the universal design principles outlined in the last chapter reduces the need for individualized supports, some children with disabilities require more specific interventions to access the curriculum, participate in activities, and make progress (Center for Parent Information and Resources 2016a). To make inclusion a reality, early childhood educators and special education professionals must work together to provide accommodations to meet each child's needs.

While the support of professionals trained in special education is vital for teaching children with delays or disabilities, teachers and child care providers must recognize and believe in their own skills when working with children. By working alongside other professionals with specialized training and building on everyone's knowledge, teachers can apply their energy and creativity to help children flourish.

Identifying the Supports Children Need

To help children be successful in the general education classroom, first identify your expectations for all children within the typical routines, activities, and lessons of the day. Doing so lets you see the barriers a child with a disability may have with access or participation, and then you can start problem-solving to remove those barriers and meet children's specific needs. Begin by considering simple curricular modifications you can make.

Curricular Modifications

Researchers Sandall and Schwartz (2008) identified several simple curricular modifications as part of what they call the "building blocks" needed to promote high-quality inclusive practices and improve educational outcomes for children with disabilities. With the foundation of high-quality early childhood classrooms as the first building block, you can add one or more of these curricular modifications to change a routine, activity, or material and provide children with greater access and participation. Sandall and Schwartz (2008) identify eight curricular modifications:

1. **Environmental supports:** Alter the physical or social environment to encourage children's participation, engagement, and learning. For example, label baskets, folders, or shelves so students know where materials go when they are done with them. To help a child transition to a new activity, give him a picture or symbol of the area showing where he should go next.

2. **Materials adaptations:** Make changes to the way a child holds or uses a material so she can be more independent. Add grips to make pencils, crayons, or markers easier to handle.

3. **Simplify the activity:** Break a task into smaller steps, or change or reduce the number of steps the child does on her own. For example, help a child put on her coat and engage the zipper, then have the child pull the zipper up so she finishes the activity with success.

4. **Child preferences:** Add something a child enjoys to interest him in participating in an activity. If he loves music, find ways to incorporate songs and rhythms into daily routines and activities.

5. **Special equipment:** Provide equipment and devices that make it easier for a child to participate. This might be loop scissors or specialized technology like touchscreens or large keyboards.

6. **Adult support:** Have an adult take part in an activity to support the child as necessary. For example, follow alongside the child in an outdoor obstacle course, prompting him to do the next step only when he needs prompting.

7. **Peer support:** Use a child's peers as models or to support the child during activities only when he needs it. For example, assign everyone a buddy, partnering children who have a delay or disability with their same-age peers. Buddies can model what to do during a game or activity for the children with disabilities and provide minimal support as needed.

8. **Invisible support:** Intentionally plan or arrange the order of when children participate. For example, arrange for a child who has difficulty waiting to take her turn early during a group activity. When you ask a question that has multiple answers, choose the child with a disability first if you think it will be difficult for him to think of other answers.

Implementing Additional Supports: Specially Designed Instruction and Individualized Interventions

Some children need more than these general curricular adaptations to be successful in the classroom. In these situations, the teachers and therapists write an IFSP or IEP goal that outlines a specially designed instruction or individualized intervention the child needs in order to learn a particular skill. The classroom teacher, the special education teacher, and any related service providers who work with the student are all responsible for implementing and working toward the goals listed in the child's IFSP or IEP. They also monitor and report on the child's progress toward those goals during the school year.

One of the most effective ways to work on these specialized goals is through **embedded learning** opportunities, where teachers and therapists intentionally create opportunities to work on specific goals during the classroom routines and activities, like Juan's occupational therapy in the vignette at the beginning of this chapter. These individualized interventions are specific to each child and focus on increasing his engagement and participation and targeting behaviors that

Allowing for Flexibility

Thinking back to the principles of universal design, plan lessons and design your instruction so there are multiple ways to

Present information (verbally, in writing, with diagrams and other visual aids)

Have students participate in learning (using technology, arts, manipulatives, hands-on methods)

Ask students to demonstrate what they know or have just learned (verbally, visually, in writing, using manipulatives)

help the child learn to be independent and develop healthy social relationships (McWilliam & Casey 2008).

Identifying the expectations you have for all students within the typical routines, activities, and lessons of the school day allows specialists to determine what skills a child needs to develop and where and when she needs to use them. With that knowledge, a specialist can plan multiple opportunities for the child to practice skills in the natural environment, where she most needs them (Jung 2007; McWilliam & Casey 2008; McWilliam & Scott 2001; Snyder et al. 2007). Here are a few examples of embedded interventions:

» A speech therapist custom designs a communication board and teaches a child to use it to communicate and interact with the other children, or to use it during reading time to increase the child's participation during the lesson.

» A teacher of the visually impaired works with you to add braille to classroom labels for a child who is learning to recognize and read braille. This teacher also helps you obtain a kickball with bells inside so the child can participate in games with the other children.

» An occupational therapist designs a removable grip for a specific child that can be used on pencils, markers, paintbrushes, or eating utensils to make it easier for the child to use these materials independently. The therapist also works on small motor activities with the child during center time a couple of times a week.

Embedding interventions in the classroom routines and activities is the preferred model for teaching children skills and allowing them to practice those skills. Many young children with disabilities do not easily generalize learning or transfer skills from one situation to another, so when they receive specialized interventions and therapies in clinics, professional offices, or special therapy rooms, they are not learning to use these skills in different places and in the settings they are in for most of the day (Jung 2007). Embedding interventions also helps classroom teachers (and families, when the therapy takes place at home) learn ways to support the child appropriately at times when the therapist is not there (Jung 2007; McWilliam & Casey 2007). This not only is helpful for the adults but also increases the number of opportunities the child has to practice certain skills throughout the day (Jung 2003).

Partnering with Special Education Teachers to Provide Individualized Supports

Special education teachers are valuable sources of information to other professionals and families, helping them understand how the child's impairment affects him in and out of the classroom and what adaptations, modifications, or supports may be necessary. They can also help you identify a child's strengths and interests and find ways to connect these to the learning going on in the classroom. Special education teachers specialize in adapting and modifying the curriculum, physical classroom space, materials, and educational expectations in order for children with disabilities to participate in the routines and activities of the classroom.

Children with delays or disabilities are more like their peers than different, but it is still important to understand the bigger picture when designing programs and choosing instructional strategies. To prepare to teach *all* children in your classroom—those with and without delays and disabilities (identified or not-yet identified)—you must regularly examine your practices, your beliefs about children and families, and your understanding of both child development and individual child needs. Consider how to make learning, as well as the physical environment, accessible and appropriate for children.

Asking yourself questions about your teaching on a regular basis can help you clarify what you do and why, and what changes you might make to benefit children's learning and development. Here are a few questions to consider:

1. What do the children in my program need to know?

What are the basic skills or concepts the children must know before they move on to the next grade or program? Do all of the children have some basic skills and concepts already? If so, what do they need to know next? If they do not have many, or any, of these basic skills and concepts yet, what skills and concepts do they have that I can build on?

2. How am I going to teach this unique group of children?

How can I present the skills and concepts so these children learn them? Do I need to change the way I have always taught something? Do I need to change the way I teach for certain students, but not the rest? What hands-on activities and opportunities can I provide for children to practice these concepts and skills? What resources do I have, and what others can I seek out?

3. What school-related attitudes and social behaviors am I emphasizing?

How do I use the routines, activities, and interactions in my classroom to stimulate children to love learning, be curious, persist at new experiences, and solve problems? How am I helping children fit in, make friends, be part of a group, and cooperate with others? What strategies help or hinder children's abilities to regulate their attention and emotions and make good decisions about their behavior?

4. How am I meeting the needs of each student?

How do I make sure each child feels safe and secure enough in my classroom to learn? How can I put my students' needs, including their social and emotional needs, at the center of everything I do? How can I get to know them and their families better and understand how children's home situations might be affecting what I see in the classroom? How can I engage *all* the children and motivate them to be part of the activities we do? What strategies do I already use that might work with this group of children or a particular child? What other strategies will I need, and who can help me learn them?

5. How do I know if children learn what I teach them?

What does mastery of these skills and concepts look like? Will it look the same for each child? How do I know if each child has learned them or not? How will I know if children can use these skills or concepts in other circumstances?

You may find some children to be more challenging to figure out than others, but all of them are worth your time and effort!

Special education teachers play many roles in schools and in classrooms, and due to the individualized nature of children's needs, schools must be innovative and flexible with these roles. Special education teachers may be assigned to co-teach with a general education teacher all day or for part of the day. **Co-teaching** provides the opportunity for professionals with different expertise to share teaching duties and responsibilities as well as increase the opportunity for specially designed instruction to be embedded in routines and activities.

Some special education teachers lead their own classrooms, serving only students with disabilities. Others may consult with the general education teacher on an as-needed basis to help problem-solve issues that arise in the classroom.

Partnering with Speech, Physical, and Occupational Therapists to Provide Individualized Supports

Speech, physical, and occupational therapists provide what are known as related services. These therapists usually specialize in a single area, such as language development, large motor development, or small motor development, and help design solutions for a child's specific needs in that area. Related service providers help children with disabilities learn to participate in the classroom routines, activities, and instruction. They may provide direct therapy services to the child during the school day or after school, or they may provide consultative services to the teacher, helping him problem solve and brainstorm ideas. Related service providers also supply adapted or specialized materials that help children participate in the classroom more independently.

A speech therapist, for example, might work on vocabulary with a child who has a hearing impairment and encourage the teacher to use many different words to explain concepts to help fill in vocabulary gaps the child has because she hears mostly fragmented speech. An occupational therapist might work on helping a child with autism tolerate the textures of paint or other creative media. For a student who has trouble with balance and large motor control, a physical therapist might provide a special chair for the classroom and suggest modifications for some of the activities in physical education.

Partnering with Teacher Assistants to Provide Individualized Supports

Many programs for young children have more than one adult in the classroom to help all of the children. Each state or program has different requirements for which classrooms must have a teacher assistant as well as the qualifications for this position. In each classroom, the teacher and the assistant have different roles and work together a little differently, but the teacher takes the lead in defining the day-to-day responsibilities, communicates the assistant's responsibilities to her, and is ultimately responsible for each child's education.

Teacher assistants help make the most of instruction by providing support for the classroom teacher. They support students during lessons and activities, review and practice skills a child is learning, provide behavioral support, and supervise students during routines and activities such as lunch, washing hands, recess, or naptime.

Sometimes families or staff feel that a child requires the assistance of an adult to work one-to-one with that child. This is particularly true for children who have complex needs, such as help with repositioning, feeding, and toileting.

In some cases, the provision of a one-to-one assistant for an individual student may be a good intention gone awry (Giangreco 2010). For example, a student who needs assistance only for staying on task or working on classroom assignments may be better served through other types of supports and modifications discussed in this and later chapters. In addition, children who have one-to-one assistants sometimes become dependent on adult help, hindering their motivation to be independent.

Some teachers, unclear on the role of the one-to-one assistant, unintentionally give up the bulk of responsibility of teaching and assessing the child to the assistant, who often has minimal training. In some cases, one-to-one assistants end up making educational decisions on their own because they feel they know the child the best (Giangreco 2010).

Children with disabilities, like any other child, must have their needs addressed by a certified teacher or other qualified professional (Giangreco 2013; Rutherford 2011). If an IEP team decides that a child needs individual assistance, the team might assign a one-to-one assistant on a limited or temporary basis and write specific goals designed to withdraw this support as quickly as possible.

Using Assistive Technology to Provide Individualized Supports and Interventions

While most learning for young children comes from real-life interactions with materials and people, technology is an important learning tool. Many aspects of technology, like directly touching a tablet screen to interact with an app, are considered part of universal design and offer a powerful way to increase children's access to and participation in learning. And when it is something all the other children are using, technology offers children with disabilities a chance to fit in and not feel set apart by using "special" equipment. Keep in mind, however, that you can do a lot to help foster positive attitudes and acceptance toward children who do need special equipment that looks different from what other children use. If you have a matter-of-fact attitude and accept it as just another tool for learning, so will children.

Some specialized technology, referred to as **assistive technology** (AT), is used as an individualized intervention for children who have trouble communicating. Using AT increases a child's ability to participate in the curriculum and in social situations, and it helps children make progress toward learning standards.

AT is not necessarily expensive or out of reach for your classroom. AT devices are available to children with disabilities at little or no cost to families if the children have an IFSP or IEP. Teachers or families can contact the child's service coordinator for more information.

AT includes a wide range of tools, from laminated cards to complex computers, and is commonly classified in one of three ways:

» **Low-tech or no-tech devices.** These tools have no source of power but are used as AT for young children. Low-tech devices include pictures used to communicate with others, which can be in a small photo album carried by the child, hung around the room by some reusable adhesive, or even hooked onto a ring that the child or teacher holds on to. Low-tech devices also include a slightly weighted blanket that helps a child sleep easier during naptime, or cups with straws that make it easier for a child to drink independently. There are likely many low-tech or no-tech supports you already use in your classroom without even realizing they are assistive technology.

» **Mid-tech devices.** These devices have a source of power and are designed for specific tasks. Simple switches can be added to radios or other devices that are powered by batteries, or objects such as blenders can be plugged into an environmental control unit with a switch to turn them on or off so the child can manipulate them and participate in group activities. Some easy-to-use mid-tech devices that help children communicate are known as **augmentative and alternative communication** (AAC) devices. These devices might have recorded words or phrases that are placed under pictures, and when the child presses the picture, the words or phrases are spoken by the AAC device. These devices are usually not complex and can be reprogrammed by adults so that they display different pictures.

» **High-tech devices.** Complex to use and program, these devices are usually used only by children as they get older, perhaps starting in middle school. High-tech devices include computers that store thousands of words and provide individuals with disabilities more nuanced options for communicating with others.

Determining Individualized Supports and Interventions in the Classroom

Now let's put this process of determining what a child needs into action! An activity matrix, like the ones that follow, illustrates the way professionals working with a child are part of the decision-making process in providing individualized supports and interventions in the classroom. A matrix helps you recognize routines and activities where children with disabilities need additional support to be independent, identify barriers, and outline opportunities during different times of the day to help increase a child's independence.

1. Outline the classroom routines and expectations you have for the whole class. Describe these in as much detail as possible, highlighting what a child is expected to be able to do to complete a task independently or with only occasional assistance. One of the first things this activity accomplishes is to give you a chance to review the developmental appropriateness of your practices.

2. Note the difficulties a child is facing with that particular routine or activity.

3. Identify what you and other adults who work with the child can do to change the environment or processes to enable that child to experience greater success and independence.

4. Using this information, work with the child's family, therapists, and other providers to identify functional IFSP or IEP goals for him that address each issue and that can be implemented during appropriate routines and activities.

Example: Four-year-old Jesse has been diagnosed with cerebral palsy and has limited functional use of his legs. It is difficult for him to move around the classroom, play with certain toys, and use the play equipment outside. Following is what an activity matrix for Jesse might look like.

Activity Matrix for Jesse

Arrival: Enter classroom with family member.
Take coats off independently, with occasional assistance from adult.
Place coats in cubbies. Older children hang coats on hook in back of cubby.

Difficulties child is having	Changes to environment or processes	IFSP/IEP goals
Jesse cannot independently remove his coat. His mom takes it off and hangs it in his cubby. Jesse's OT and PT feel Jesse could take off a lightweight coat and place it in his cubby independently. He would need help with a heavy winter coat. He should not be expected to hang up his coat on the hook. OT and PT will help teacher develop a procedure to teach Jesse how to take off his coat.	A staff member greets Jesse and Mom at door each morning and helps Jesse work on taking off his coat and hanging it up independently. Mom chats with a different staff member and then leaves. Assign Jesse the cubby farthest away from the door so he does not block the entrance while learning this procedure. Staff member stands between him and the rest of the classroom so he is not distracted and can be quickly redirected if necessary. Attach mesh net to the bottom 10 inches of his cubby to help coat stay in cubby.	Teacher and Mom develop a functional goal with consultation from OT and PT: *Jesse will go from being dependent on an adult to take off his coat and hang it up to independently removing coat and placing it in cubby behind the attached net at least 15 days in a row, with only minimal assistance provided on a maximum of 5 of those days. Staff will record data daily on chart above cubby.* Goal indicates Jesse's present level (needing assistance from an adult) and where teachers want him to be (independently taking off his coat and putting it in his cubby). Skill is considered mastered if performed 15 days in a row with assistance needed on only a few days. (He is only 4 years old, and many young children need help sometimes.)

Center time: Engage in child-initiated play activities.
Play with or next to peers without disturbing the play of others.
Initiate and maintain conversations about play activity with peers/adults.
Clean up materials with only occasional assistance.

Difficulties child is having	Changes to environment or processes	IFSP/IEP goals
Jesse has difficulty reaching for and getting toys from the shelves, so he rarely chooses to get toys on his own. He plays well with toys when they are put in front of him on a table, but he usually just watches the other children if he is not given toys. Jesse attempts to join in block play with some of the boys, but he sometimes accidentally knocks down their structures because of his unsteady movements. This causes some children to avoid playing with him.	With Jesse's classmates, brainstorm ways they can include Jesse in activities they like. Develop games or put out activities that require two people to play, and partner Jesse with a peer he likes. Guide the peer to get Jesse to participate. Rearrange the room so the centers have some high-demand toys available at tables, where Jesse and his friends can sit and play together. Modify some of the blocks. Add Velcro strips so the blocks stay together even if he is unsteady when he plays with them. Add a small table or ledge to the block area so Jesse can sit and play there and the other children can kneel at it.	An IEP goal may not be needed if the changes to the classroom and the blocks help Jesse play more independently. If Jesse continues to refrain from initiating play and just watches other children, develop a goal: *Jesse will go from primarily watching other children in the class play to initiating and maintaining a play activity with a peer for an increasing amount of time up to 10 minutes. Classroom staff will collect data twice a week using a timer or clock and will record the data on a collection sheet.*

Activity Matrix for Jesse (continued)

Morning meeting: At signal, gather on rug for morning meeting. Participate in songs, finger plays, and sharing news.

Difficulties child is having	Changes to environment or processes	IFSP/IEP goals
Jesse has a special low chair for morning meeting, provided by his PT. This chair allows him to sit on the floor and be at the same level as his classmates. Jesse participates with the other children in songs, finger plays, and sharing news.	Jesse's physical needs are met by his chair. No other changes need to be made during the routine at this time.	No IEP goal is needed at this time.

Small group instruction: Work at table in groups of four to five on teacher-directed learning or assessment activity. Complete task as independently as possible.

Difficulties child is having	Changes to environment or processes	IFSP/IEP goals
Jesse has little difficulty during this routine. The teacher prepares specific activities and assessments that are designed for Jesse and makes modifications to the activity so he can be as independent as possible.	No changes are necessary at this time.	This is a good time for the teacher to work on Jesse's IEP goals with him or assess him on specific skills identified in the IEP.

Snack/lunch: Manipulate food containers (milk carton/straws) with occasional assistance. Use individual utensils (spoon/fork/knife) with occasional assistance. Clean up with occasional assistance.

Difficulties child is having	Changes to environment or processes	IFSP/IEP goals
Jesse's mom sends his snack and lunch since he is a picky eater. The containers his mom uses are difficult for him to open independently, so he waits for a teacher to open them. Jesse uses a fork but not a spoon, and he does not have any experience using a knife. Since Jesse finds it difficult to walk and hold his trash without dropping it, the classroom staff brings the garbage can to him so he can throw out his trash independently.	After consulting with the OT, Jesse's mom has agreed to put his food in containers that are easier for him to open. The OT will work with Jesse during snack time to develop ways for him to be more independent and to introduce him to using a knife. The OT will try a weighted spoon to see if it helps Jesse use it more independently. Jesse's mom will send in pudding (his favorite) during snack time to encourage him to use the new spoon. The pudding is less likely to fall off the spoon, offering Jesse more opportunities to be successful.	The environmental adaptations and embedded therapies should be enough to help Jesse become more independent in this routine. No IEP goal is needed at this time.

Activity Matrix for Jesse (continued)

Whole group story time: Attend to story with occasional assistance.

Answer questions, identify rhyming words, and recognize letters/numbers with occasional assistance.

Use a variety of materials (felt pieces, props, books) to retell story with occasional assistance.

Difficulties child is having	Changes to environment or processes	IFSP/IEP goals
Jesse currently has no difficulties during this time of day.	This routine is working for Jesse as long as the materials for retelling are easy for him to manipulate and within his reach.	No IEP goal is needed at this time.
Jesse uses the same chair he uses in morning meeting to sit on the carpet and listen to a story. He attends to stories and engages in group conversation about them.		
Jesse can use different materials to retell the story when they are physically easy to manipulate and the teacher or another child places them within his reach.		

Outdoor play: Use outdoor equipment and materials as intended (climb, pedal, steer) with occasional assistance.

Difficulties child is having	Changes to environment or processes	IFSP/IEP goals
This is the hardest part of the day for Jesse.	Have the OT evaluate the outdoor play space and work with the teacher to design activities that Jesse and his classmates can do together.	The environmental adaptations and the embedded therapies should be enough to help Jesse become more independent in this routine.
The teachers put Jesse in a wagon and pull him around the playground, but that is the only thing that ever occurs to include him in this time of day. Sometimes Jesse has pull-out therapy in the PT room during large motor outdoor play. If Jesse does go outside, he primarily watches the other children play.	Jesse's PT sessions should occur during outdoor time, and the skills need to be embedded during play.	No IEP goal is needed at this time.
	The PT will show the teachers how to apply the methods and procedures she uses to help Jesse participate so they can continue to provide this instruction and assistance on the days Jesse does not work with the PT.	

Add other times of the day—such as transitions or departure time—to this matrix as needed, and include family members and all staff who work with the child regularly in conversations and decisions. Everyone has something to contribute to this process—including the child!

Example: Liam is a 3-month-old child who has been diagnosed with torticollis, a muscular problem that makes it difficult for him to turn his head or neck. Liam receives physical therapy twice a week. The physical therapist also shares ideas with Liam's family and child care providers.

Activity Matrix for Liam

Feeding: Liam is bottle-fed by the staff with the breast milk his mom brings from home.

Difficulties child is having	Changes to environment or processes	IFSP/IEP goals
Liam tilts his head to one side and does not like to feed when the left side of his body is next to the person feeding him since that stretches his neck. He gets very fussy until he is moved to face the other way.	Caregivers will keep track of which side Liam is feeding on and switch sides every time he eats. He may need more time for feeding.	*Liam will increase his tolerance for holding his head in different positions when bottle-fed.*

Playtime: Liam is put on his tummy on the floor to interact with toys and other infants.

Difficulties child is having	Changes to environment or processes	IFSP/IEP goals
Liam does not enjoy tummy time and cries until picked up.	Tummy time gently helps stretch neck muscles, which Liam needs. His caregivers will use surfaces other than the floor to help him tolerate tummy time more easily, like across the caregiver's lap or propped on a pillow. Caregivers will use Liam's favorite toys with sounds to encourage him to turn his head at times other than feeding.	*Liam will stay on his tummy at least 15 minutes at a time, 4 times per day. Until Liam can tolerate it better, shorter intervals can be used in the morning, with increased tummy time throughout the day.*

....

Teachers use a variety of supports for children with disabilities. Curricular modifications often are small changes to the environment, activities, or materials that can significantly boost a child's access and participation. Most children with disabilities also need specialized, individualized supports. The team of professionals supporting the child—including the classroom teacher, the special education or early intervention teacher, therapists, teaching assistant, and administrators—and the family all have a role in helping the child be successful in the classroom.

5 Addressing Challenging Behavior

There are times when all children behave in ways that are not easy to deal with. Every young child has times of fussiness or outbursts as he asserts his independence, tests boundaries, and learns to communicate with others. When toddlers lack the language they need to tell adults what they want (food, a toy, attention), it is not unusual for them to use tantrums, or perhaps even biting, for a short time to express their wants and needs. Most adults are not overly concerned about these kinds of behaviors because they happen infrequently and are often easy to stop or redirect for most children.

As children mature and parents and teachers model and teach effective ways of communicating and handling strong emotions, most children develop the necessary skills to interact with others and control their impulses. For some children, however, challenging behaviors are more intense, longer lasting, or more frequent than expected for their age, and this can interfere with learning and social relationships.

Many children without disabilities exhibit challenging behavior, and many with disabilities do not. If a child with a delay or disability is exhibiting challenging behavior, it is not necessarily linked to their delay or disability. Understanding *why* the behavior is occurring and looking at the behavior in the context of what you know about the child and about children's development in general enables you to support the development of skills the child may be missing (how to appropriately get an adult's attention, how to communicate frustration in non-hurting ways) and, ultimately, more appropriate behavior.

What Challenging Behavior Is Saying

Understanding several basic ideas about difficult behavior in young children can help you understand why it is occurring, which is the foundation for helping to change it.

Behavior is always a form of communication. Everyone communicates something through their behavior, most of the time without realizing it. Both positive behavior and challenging behavior express something about us and the way we are feeling at that moment.

There is *always* a reason for challenging behavior. Children use challenging behavior for one of two reasons: to get something they want (such as a toy another child is playing with) or to avoid something they *don't* want (like having to engage in a difficult task).

Challenging behaviors continue because they are effective. Young children continue to use challenging behavior because it gets them what they want or lets them avoid what they don't want. If it didn't work, they would not continue to engage in it. It may take longer to work sometimes, but as long as a behavior helps children achieve their goal, they will continue to use it.

Challenging behavior often indicates that a child lacks skills in some area. Unless you understand the reason for a behavior and address it, the child will not learn what he *should* do instead of the behavior. For example, if a child throws something because he is upset that a step in the daily routine was skipped and he cannot communicate this in any other way, he does not learn what he should do the next time this situation occurs if you simply remove him from the situation and take away a privilege. In addition, a new challenging behavior may replace the first one. You may be able to stop the throwing, but he may start kicking instead. You must identify what the child is trying to communicate and teach him how to express himself in ways that are more acceptable and that still allow him to achieve his goal. Focus on teaching those missing skills rather than getting a behavior to stop.

If you focus only on reducing a behavior, you may be removing the only way a child knows how to communicate with you (Neidert 2013). Help children learn positive, effective ways to express themselves, communicate their needs, and regulate their feelings and actions.

Changing Challenging Behavior

There are many reasons challenging behavior occurs, but in every case, the child has a specific reason or function for exhibiting that particular challenging behavior. Understanding the function of a behavior is key to changing it. To begin, look for ABC:

> » **A**ntecedent, or what happens just before the behavior starts
> » **B**ehavior, or what the behavior looks like, described in observable, measurable terms ("kicked chair five times" instead of "had temper tantrum")
> » **C**onsequence, or what happens just after the behavior ends (TCDD 2013)

Conducting a **functional behavioral assessment** (FBA) using ABC helps you identify and understand the real reason a behavior is occurring and decide how to replace the challenging behavior with more acceptable behavior. Often, this is accomplished by teaching skills the child has not yet developed. Let's consider August, a 3-year-old child in a public preschool program.

August does not have many toys at home, especially blocks, so he loves to play with the blocks at school. He loves to build big structures and, until recently, has played in the block area with other children without any problems. Lately, August has been getting angry when he plays in the block area and will knock down other children's structures, throw blocks at the other children, and scream at them until they leave the area. August's teachers feel that he does not want anyone else using the blocks and is using the behavior to scare other children away.

The teachers have also noticed that August's speech and language skills are not as developed as the other children's. They have started to use picture cards with August to help him get his meaning across to both them and to his peers.

August's teachers decide to conduct an FBA to see if there is another reason behind these behaviors besides his limited language skills and not wanting to share materials. FBA consists of the following steps:

1. Identify and describe the behavior in observable and measurable terms.

Behaviors like biting are observable and measurable; different people can agree on what biting looks like and count how many times it occurs. Descriptors like "acting out" or "being difficult" do not provide observable and measurable behaviors; not everyone agrees on what those behaviors look like, so you cannot necessarily count how many times a child is being difficult.

August's behaviors:

- Knocking down other children's block structures
- Throwing blocks at other children
- Yelling "Leave my blocks alone!" to the other children

2. Collect data.

Data collection is necessary to document the behavior—specifically looking at the ABC of the behavior. Without accurate data, you may never discover the true reason behind it or know if the behavior is really gone. The child may stop throwing blocks, but he may start pushing other children. The behavior isn't gone, it just changed. Collecting data takes time and requires your undivided attention on the child, so work with another adult to help you with this step.

Data collected on August in the block area:

- On Monday, August played in the block area with two other boys for about 15 minutes. One boy's foot bumped into August's tower and it fell. August yelled at the boy and threw blocks at both boys until the teacher intervened.

- On Tuesday, August played in the block area for 30 minutes with three classmates building a zoo. There were no issues or incidents.

- On Wednesday, August played by himself in the block area, building a tall tower. While putting a block on the top, August's elbow hit the tower and sent it crashing to the ground. He started throwing blocks at two classmates who were playing in the nearby dramatic play area until the teacher came over to stop him.

- On Thursday, August and one other boy each worked on building a tall structure. Although no one was near August's tower (not even August), it fell, causing him to yell and throw blocks at the other boy playing with him until the teacher came over.

- On Friday, August and two other boys played in the block area building midsized towers for a fort. They played together for 20 minutes with no incidents.

These observations clearly show teachers the ABC of August's behavior:

> A: August's block structure—specifically, a *tall* structure—falls

> B: August yells and throws blocks

> C: Children leave the block area, and the teacher comes over to August

3. Develop a hypothesis or hypotheses.

Look at the data you've collected and determine the function of the child's behavior. What is the child using the behavior for?

» **To get something**, including an object, a person, a preferred activity, attention from adults or peers, or a preferred sensory stimulation, like being rocked or held by an adult

» **To get away from something**, including demands, activities, people, social interactions, or non-preferred sensory stimulation (pain or discomfort) (TACSEI 2011)

Hypothesis for August:

August's teachers think he is trying to get something when he yells and throws blocks. His behavior occurs when his block tower falls. He is having difficulty building a very tall tower on his own and getting the blocks to be stable. He gets frustrated and yells and throws blocks when he cannot make the tower stable. His behavior is communicating to the teachers that he needs help in learning how to make a tall tower more stable.

4. Develop and implement a behavior intervention plan.

A **behavior intervention plan** (BIP) is a plan that's based on the hypothesis you develop through the FBA process. The BIP is designed to teach a child missing skills or replacement behaviors that are more appropriate and that the child can reasonably be expected to learn at this stage of his development. The plan should also include reinforcing the child's use of the appropriate replacement skill (Chazin & Ledford 2016). Include the child in the development of the plan as much as you can. Ask him what he wants to see happen to make it better—what he comes up with may surprise you!

Behavior intervention plan for August:

1. Modify the environment: Help August learn how to make a tall tower by building it against the wall, which will provide some stability. Glue felt onto some of the blocks to make them more likely to stick together and not slide around.

2. Teach August what to do if the tower falls on its own or if someone knocks it over: If his tower falls, August will tell a teacher what happened, and the teacher will reinforce this behavior by giving August an opportunity to build the tower again, even if the rest of the class is doing something else. She will offer to take a picture of the new tower with the class tablet and email the photo to his dad. (Taking a photo is August's idea.)

3. Provide another way for August to communicate when he gets angry and engages in this behavior: Give him some picture cards that identify his feelings (sad, angry, frustrated) and that describe what he can do next (I need help, I want to rebuild). Teaching August to communicate what he is feeling may help de-escalate some of the outbursts.

5. Gather additional data.

Once you have started an intervention, continue collecting data to see whether the intervention is working or you need to adjust something. This part takes time, and change will not happen overnight. You may not have correctly identified the behavior's function, indicating that your replacement skills are not correct and that you need to rethink your hypothesis.

More data on August:

- Week 1: August spent two days with the teacher learning how to build block towers against the wall, but he decided that he did not want to do it that way. August liked the blocks with the felt and wanted to make sure that no one else used them. The teacher put these special blocks in a basket labeled with his name and also made a few more blocks for anyone else who wanted to use them. There were three incidents during the week where August threw blocks and yelled at his peers in the block area when his tower fell over. The teacher modeled for him how to tell her what happened, and then she gave him time to build another tower with her. They took a photo of the tower and emailed it to August's dad.

- Week 2: There were still three yelling incidents during the week but no block throwing. While yelling at his classmates, August came over to tell the teacher what happened. The teacher modeled for him how to come and tell her what happened without yelling, and then gave him time to build another tower with her. They took a photo and emailed it to August's dad.

- Week 3: There was one incident where August threw a block at a classmate who knocked down his tower, but he quickly went on to rebuild the tower by himself without telling the teacher. He finished the tower before it was time to leave the block area. He did not request to take a photo of the blocks this week.

- Week 4: There were no incidents of throwing blocks or yelling at peers this week. On one occasion, August asked for extra time to rebuild his tower that had fallen and requested that the teacher take a photo to send to his dad.

Conducting an FBA and writing a BIP based on the information you collect is the best way to help a child learn the skills he is missing and to prevent behaviors that arise from this lack of skills. Once you understand the real reason for the behavior, you may find it relatively easy to replace those challenging behaviors with positive ones. Collecting data lets you know whether the plan is working, even if it is in very small steps. Realize that a behavior may actually increase after you start trying to replace it before it decreases. Be consistent in applying your intervention, and remember to recognize and reinforce the new behavior.

Sometimes there are other reasons for challenging behavior that make it difficult to understand and resolve, such as medical issues (earaches) or changes at home (new baby, loss of a parent's job). If behaviors are not diminishing, step back and look for a new

Children react to and process stressful experiences and trauma differently than adults do, and when these experiences occur during the first five years of life, they significantly impact a child's social and emotional well-being (Center on the Developing Child 2013). Research (Cooper, Masi, & Vick 2009) indicates that

- Almost 9 percent of children who receive mental health services in the United States are younger than 6 years old.
- Young children under the age of 5 may experience more severe mental health disorders that require interventions from trained mental health professionals. These professionals also work directly with families and the child's school (with parental consent) to help them provide consistent interventions.

Even from a very young age, some children exhibit mental health disorders like anxiety disorder, conduct disorder, depression, eating disorders, and post-traumatic stress disorder, and these disorders impact their social and emotional development as well as their ability to learn (Center on the Developing Child 2013). Trauma can impact a child's mental health enough to have lasting effects, and children may never fully recover psychologically (Center on the Developing Child 2013). Stress—including certain life circumstances like extreme and persistent poverty, unsafe neighborhoods, and domestic violence as well as persistent physical or emotional abuse and neglect—elevates a child's risk of mental health disorders (Kieffer 2016). Even when a child is removed from an abusive or neglectful situation, she is likely to have problems with self-regulation and relating to others (Vann 2011).

Diagnosing mental health disorders in children is more difficult than diagnosing them in adults and is done by a child or adolescent psychologist or psychiatrist. Pediatricians, as well as professionals in hospitals and community mental health clinics, can perform basic mental health screenings and refer families to appropriate mental health professionals for further evaluation and treatment (Center on the Developing Child 2013; Cooper, Masi, & Vick 2009; Nelson & Mann 2011).

hypothesis or a connection you've missed. Behavior is a puzzle, and puzzles are not always solved on the first try!

Preventing Challenging Behavior

Prevention strategies can address many of the challenging behaviors children exhibit. Often, you can prevent some challenging behaviors by changing your practices.

Changing Classroom Environments, Routines, Schedules, and Transitions

» Have a consistent basic schedule and regular routines. A predictable routine helps children understand what to expect next, which makes them more relaxed and cooperative as well as independent.

» Make sure all materials and activities are developmentally appropriate (and accessible) to foster independence. Providing appropriate choices so children have some control over their activities encourages initiative and independence and helps them focus on learning.

» Reduce the number of transitions a child has to make each day, and have a routine around each transition (like a song) so you can teach her how to transition and what your expectations are. For example, sing the expectations of a transition ("If you're finished cleaning up, choose a book!") to the tune of "If You're Happy and You Know It." Model and have her practice choosing a book to look at when she's finished cleaning up after center time.

Using the Power of Peers

» Use peers to model appropriate social behavior.

» Set up the classroom routines and activities so they support peer buddies (line up together, talk to your partner about your answers, have a lunchroom buddy).

» Choose buddies intentionally; some children make better partners than others. Do not always choose the most socially advanced child; look for one who is sensitive to the overall skills of a child with a disability.

Teaching Social and Emotional Skills

» Model taking turns, sharing, and other social skills, such as comforting a classmate who is upset.

» Teach children how to problem solve and negotiate when sharing materials.

» As a group, come up with no more than three to six clear classroom rules that state what children *should* do, rather than what they should *not* do (for example, "Use gentle touches" instead of "No hitting").

» Teach the rules and have children practice them in context.

» Have clear consequences for not following the rules, and enforce them fairly and consistently with all children.

» Acknowledge and reinforce appropriate behaviors and positive child interactions ("Keyonte, that was kind of you to pick up Devon's marker for her"). Catch children being good!

....

A child with a delay or a disability is a child who has the same needs as other children do, including the need for an education. Education is a human right and should be accessible for every child without discrimination (UNICEF 2009). Part 1 of this book is meant to help teachers understand the language and terms that are used in special education or when describing children with delays or disabilities as well as the larger concepts about working with children with delays or disabilities.

While disabilities impact each child in a different way, Part 2 of this book offers some definitions and general indications of common impairments to help teachers be more knowledgeable when they suspect that a child in their classroom may have a delay or disability. Part 2 also provides some practical suggestions for helping a child with a potential or an identified delay or disability communicate, interact, and learn.

Specific Disabilities

7 Autism Spectrum Disorder

Four-year-old Jasper, diagnosed with autism spectrum disorder at age 2, is fascinated with trains. He spends hours playing with them at home and at school. He loves to watch YouTube videos about trains, and he talks about trains to anyone who will listen. Jasper gets especially excited when his grandmother takes him to visit the train station near her house.

Jasper's preschool teacher, Ms. Durand, wants to expand his interests and encourage him to play with other children, so she considers making the classroom a train-free zone. She could put away the classroom train set so it does not distract Jasper and ask Jasper's mom not to let him bring any trains to school.

When Ms. Durand talks about her idea with the special education coordinator, Mrs. Mosley, Mrs. Mosley explains that this strategy would probably not be effective in encouraging Jasper to engage in other types of play or talk about other topics. In fact, removing trains from the classroom is likely to lead to a power struggle. If Jasper brings a train to school and the teacher takes it away, he could become extremely upset and throw a tantrum.

Ms. Durand thinks about what Mrs. Mosley has said. Upon further reflection, she realizes that trying to force Jasper to abandon his interest and play with a variety of toys and materials is not developmentally appropriate. She also remembers that a child's interests can be used as positive teaching tools to calm and motivate the child as well as improve learning.

With this in mind, Ms. Durand, in consultation with his parents, decides to use Jasper's interest in trains as a springboard for him to engage in the everyday routines and activities of the classroom. She adds books about trains to the library area, and as she hopes, this encourages Jasper to spend more time reading. In the art area, she includes trains and photos of trains to encourage Jasper to draw or paint train-related pictures, like the station he visits with his grandmother, or to push the wheels of a train through clay and notice the tracks it makes. Ms. Durand also helps him set up a speed-testing area so he and his classmates can race the trains down inclines. Since Jasper also is very interested in stopwatches, she puts him in charge of measuring the time for each train. He announces the time

to another child, who then records it on a chart. Soon, Jasper shows interest in recording the times himself.

As some of the other children gradually begin to get involved in these activities, learning about trains together helps Jasper make some new friends. As the year goes on, Jasper's fascination with trains continues, but Ms. Durand is gratified to see from her informal assessments that his skills in several areas have improved thanks to this strategy.

There is a saying that if you have met one person with autism . . . you have met *one* person with autism. Children and adults with autism spectrum disorder (ASD) have different behaviors and levels of severity, and the disorder impacts each person in different ways. Although people with ASD may share some of the same characteristics—like Jasper, above, they may have an intense interest in a particular area or object—each individual is unique. So, too, are the ways teachers and families interact with children with ASD and the interventions they provide.

What Is Autism Spectrum Disorder?

ASD is a group of neurodevelopmental disorders that have a wide range of characteristics (Autism Speaks 2012; Contie 2007). ASD affects children's behavior, communication, cognitive ability, and social skills (NINDS 2015). Although the terms *autism* and *Asperger*

ASD by the numbers

In the 1980s, the CDC quoted the number of people with autism as approximately 4 in 10,000 people. In 2007 that number was 1 in 88 people, and in 2013 it was 1 in 50 people—a 72 percent increase in 5 years (CDC 2016a).

syndrome are no longer officially used (the *Diagnostic and Statistical Manual of Mental Disorders,* 5th edition, uses *autism spectrum disorder*), many schools, families, and advocacy groups continue to use them. ASD is diagnosed in all racial and ethnic groups, and it is almost five times more likely to be diagnosed in boys than in girls (CDC 2016a).

Risk Factors for Autism Spectrum Disorder

ASD is so complex that researchers believe there are multiple causes of the disorder (CDC 2016b), but what those causes are remains unknown. There is no single gene responsible for ASD, and it is likely that both genetic and environmental factors are involved (Mayo Clinic 2014a). Several factors make it more likely that a child will develop ASD (CDC 2016a; NIMH 2016):

» Gender—boys are more likely to develop ASD than girls

» A sibling or other family member with ASD

» Premature birth and/or low birth weight

» Older parents

» A genetic or chromosomal disorder, such as fragile X syndrome

Ongoing research may identify additional factors and provide a more thorough understanding of the causes of ASD (CDC 2016a).

The Rise in the Prevalence of ASD

While the exact number of ASD diagnoses is difficult to track, the overall trend has increased dramatically over the past few decades (CDC 2016a). There are several theories on what is contributing to this increase in the number of individuals, both children and adults, diagnosed with ASD. Many professionals in the medical and autism advocacy communities believe that the increase may be due to a combination of three indirect factors: better awareness of the condition, changes in the definition and expansion of the criteria that define ASD, and a shift in diagnosis (Hansen, Schendel, & Parner 2014).

Although the prevalence of ASD has increased dramatically, the overall percentage of children who receive services for intellectual, behavioral, and social skills problems has remained basically unchanged for many years. A study found that children who in the past would have been diagnosed with an intellectual disability are now more likely to be diagnosed with autism spectrum disorder (Sholtis 2015). The study evaluated state special education data for students educated in programs under IDEA between 2000 and 2010 and found a nearly 65 percent increase in the number of students with ASD during that time. This corresponded with a nearly 65 percent decrease in the number of students identified as having an intellectual disability (Sholtis 2015). This suggests that the rise in prevalence of ASD may be at least partially due to a shift in diagnosis.

Impact of ASD on Development and Learning

Children with ASD are affected in different ways and to different degrees by the disorder. They commonly show the following characteristics (NIMH 2016):

» Difficulty with social communication and interaction across many different situations and with different people

» Limited interests and repetitive actions and behaviors

» Difficulty functioning in the daily environment

» Symptoms present before age 2

A child with ASD may show little interest in other people, not making much eye contact and appearing not to listen when others talk. She may have difficulty understanding social cues and facial expressions. While most young children understand that others have different emotions and thoughts than they do, a child with ASD may not grasp this. Changes in routine—the daily schedule, a new person picking her up from preschool—may cause a child to become very upset. Sounds or visual stimuli that other children may hardly notice can be very bothersome to a child with ASD. Engaging in repetitive behaviors, such as rocking or twirling, is common. A child with ASD may show great interest in a certain area, like numbers or details on a certain subject, and may talk incessantly on these topics. Some things might come very easily to her, like using a computer, but she might find it difficult to make friends.

Although there is no cure for ASD, and although some children with ASD struggle more than others do with social interaction, academics, and behavior, almost every child will progress in each of these areas over time. Some need more assistance during the preschool years than they will need in the primary grades. Some will struggle with academics in the early primary grades but will have less difficulty in later grades. While many children with ASD have intellectual disabilities, many others have above-average cognitive abilities and excel in certain areas.

Identifying Autism Spectrum Disorder

To determine whether a child has ASD, a doctor looks at the child's behavior, language, motor development, family history, and his parents' observations. Information from other professionals, such as a child psychologist or therapist, may also be involved in the diagnostic process. Two specific categories of signs professionals look for are repetitive behaviors and difficulty with social interactions (Autism Speaks 2017; Filipek et al. 2000).

No Link Between Vaccines and ASD

Some individuals have expressed concern that vaccines, specifically the measles, mumps, and rubella (MMR) vaccine, can cause ASD in some children. Since vaccines are designed to protect children from preventable diseases, a significant amount of research has been conducted on the relationship between vaccines and ASD. From this research, the Centers for Disease Control and Prevention (CDC), the American Academy of Pediatrics (AAP), and the World Health Organization (WHO) have concluded that vaccines, including those with mercury-based preservatives like thimerisol, do not cause ASD (Taylor, Swerdfeger, & Eslick 2014). (Thimerisol is no longer used in vaccines for children [CDC 2015b].) Parents who are concerned about the safety of vaccines or the vaccination schedule for their child should consult with their child's doctor to obtain the most current information.

Demonstrating specific, repetitive behaviors:

» Tend not to make eye contact with people

» Tend not to pay attention to people around them

» Do not usually respond when their name is called

» Do not usually want to interact with other people by playing with them or showing them what they are playing with

Having trouble with everyday social interactions:

» Are overly focused on, or even obsessed with, one specific toy and have difficulty shifting focus

» Tend to line up or organize toys in a specific way rather than play with them in a variety of ways

» Insist on the same routine and schedule every day, such as eating the same foods or touching a favorite toy once before he goes to sleep every night; inconsolable if the routine is changed in any way

Parents and professionals generally notice ASD behaviors before a child is 18 months old. The CDC recommends that doctors screen for ASD at well-child visits when children are 18 and 24 months. By the time a child is 2 or 3 years old, many experienced doctors are comfortable making this diagnosis (Filipek 2000).

Diagnosing Older Children with ASD

Not all children are diagnosed with ASD when they are very young. A child's symptoms may be mild or not readily apparent, and formal diagnosis may not be completed until the child is school age. Older children who may have ASD might have difficulty with the following (Raising Children Network 2016):

» Taking turns in conversations, preferring to do all the talking

» Answering questions about themselves

» Talking about a range of topics; many have a favorite topic they want to talk about all the time

Red Flags

According to Autism Speaks (2017), the following signs may indicate that a child is at risk for ASD:

- No big smiles or other warm, joyful expressions by 6 months or thereafter

- No back-and-forth sharing of sounds, smiles, or other facial expressions by 9 months

- No babbling by 12 months

- No back-and-forth gestures such as pointing, showing, reaching, or waving by 12 months

- No words by 16 months

- No meaningful two-word phrases (not including imitating or repeating) by 24 months

- Any loss of speech, babbling, or social skills at any age

If a child exhibits any of these behaviors, families should be encouraged to see their doctor.

» Interpreting body language

» Understanding expressions like "knock it off," tending to take these literally

» Modulating their voice, tending to speak in a strange pitch or monotone

» Following directions with more than one or two steps

Strategies for the Classroom

Children with ASD have widely varying strengths and challenges, and teaching strategies need to be individualized to meet those unique needs. Classroom teachers work with special education professionals to choose and implement a specific methodology or program (called an intervention) that will provide children with the skills they need to be successful in school and everyday activities. These interventions must be proven to be effective with children who have ASD. Interventions that meet this standard of effectiveness are called **evidence-based practices** (EBPs), and both IDEA and the Every Student Succeeds Act (ESSA) of 2015 (Public Law 114-95) require schools and programs to use interventions that are proven effective by scientifically based research.

While no single intervention works for every child, several are effective with children with ASD (NAC 2015). Commonly used approaches include the following:

» **Applied behavior analysis (ABA).** ABA programs focus on breaking down skills into small, distinct steps, teaching a small step, and immediately rewarding the child when he masters it. This use of instantaneous positive reinforcement increases the likelihood that the child will repeat the skill. High-quality ABA programs do not follow a specific curriculum, program, set of drills, or assessment, and they are not a one-size-fits-all approach.

» **Peer training programs.** Peer training programs, or peer-based interventions, teach peers how to initiate and respond during social interactions with a child with ASD. Peers learn how to get the attention of the child with ASD, provide assistance, model appropriate play skills, organize play activities, and other actions. An example of a peer training program is the LEAP model—Learning Experiences: An Alternative Program for Preschoolers and Parents.

Formal interventions like ABA may seem intimidating, but there are many strategies you can use in your everyday routines, activities, and lessons to help children with ASD.

Here are some simple ideas to try with a very young child who has ASD or who exhibits similar behaviors:

» Give clear directions: "Put two toys in the bin. Then, we can eat."

» Follow a specific routine before naptime each day, such as the child finding his favorite soft toy to nap with, turning off the lights in the room, and lying down to listen to one story.

» Work with a child's family to understand the child's routines at home and other places in the community he goes with his family and the supports the family provides. Provide similar routines and supports at school so the child experiences consistency.

With preschoolers, consider these strategies (ACF & NICHD 2013):

» **Engage children in social play.** For a child with limited play skills, directly teach him how to play with a partner by taking turns with an object, such as rolling a ball back and forth with someone. Encourage him to look at the object and talk to his

Inclusion of Children with ASD

Where young children with ASD are taught may be a more important factor than the particular intervention used. The need for specialized interventions does not negate the mandate for all children with disabilities to be educated in the least restrictive environment and should not be the driving factor when deciding placement (Koegel et al. 2012). Indeed, many interventions are most effective when children participate in an inclusive setting, where teachers can facilitate social participation and social learning with their peers (Winton 2016). Being educated alongside their peers is an essential part of helping children with ASD imitate and learn age-appropriate academic, behavioral, and social skills. Children

with ASD who have not had many opportunities for inclusion in the preschool years tend to experience greater social exclusion and isolation in the primary grades (Bottema-Beutel et al. 2017; Gasser, Malti, & Buholzer 2014). When teachers focus on increasing high-quality interactions in preschool and the primary grades, children with ASD are more likely to be socially accepted and have friends when they are older (Bottema-Beutel et al. 2017; Gasser, Malti, & Buholzer 2014). Building social skills while young helps to ensure that children will be a vital part of other environments—school, recreation, and community—as they grow older.

partner. This kind of play helps children to attend to the same object or activity as another person and make social connections.

» **Teach peers how to play with a child with ASD.** Showing the other children in class how to initiate play with a child with ASD makes it more likely that the child with ASD will develop friendships, learn appropriate social skills, and feel included as a full member of the classroom. For example, teach peers how to model pretending to feed the baby doll, hand off the baby doll and the bottle to the child with ASD, and help her feed the baby too.

» **Use favorite toys to help with transitions.** Use a child's favorite toy to help her transition to an activity that she does not prefer. For example, when it is time to leave the classroom and board the school bus, pretend the child's prized doll stroller is rolling down the sidewalk toward the bus.

» **Give them a social job.** Give a child with ASD a simple job to do every day that gives him meaningful interactions with peers, such as giving napkins to everyone before snack. Teach the child how to pass out a napkin to each person, and once he understands the expectations of the job, teach him how to interact with the other children as he does this. For example, he might ask each child, "Would you like a napkin?"

» **Use visual schedules and provide visual choices.** Using a daily schedule with photos or drawings and words gives the child a concrete idea of what will happen next. Offer limited visual choices of which activity she wants to do next to give the child some control over transitions without overwhelming her. For example, show her a picture of someone reading a book and a picture of someone using the computer and ask her which activity she wants to do.

Children with ASD in the early primary grades can be supported through these strategies:

» **Teach children routines for social interaction.** For example, to help the child introduce himself to others, make two cue cards, one with the child's photo and the words "My name is Misha," and the other with a stop sign to remind him to wait for a response. Practice this routine several times with a group of children.

» **Use a child's preferences to increase his motivation to complete activities.** For example, if Roberto has trouble completing math assignments, after he completes three problems correctly, he gets five minutes on the computer or a short break—whichever is a reinforcer for him. Families can help you determine what their children find motivating (and remember that what is reinforcing may change over time).

» **Expand a child's interests.** If a child's interest or fascination is not age appropriate, introduce the child to other materials that are, like the newest toy or gadget that is popular for children her age. This lets her share an interest with same-age peers and have something to talk about with them.

» **Modify assignments.** Have a peer support the child during science experiments, or let the child type her responses instead of writing them.

For all ages, keep in mind the need to

» Provide structure and a consistent routine. If something needs to change, alert the child ahead of time whenever possible.

» Keep visual and auditory distractions to a minimum. Don't expect a child to listen to two people at once. Remember that a child with ASD may be either under- or oversensitive to lights and noise.

» Make directions short and concrete. For example, "Put your blue folder in the blue box on the table."

» Provide a quiet place where children can go when they need to be alone for a while.

Summary

While there is no specific cause identified yet, researchers and education professionals are learning more every day about how ASD impacts development and how to intervene early to help children make progress.

The interventions used to teach young children with ASD must be backed by research, and research continues to refine those methods. Appropriate educational settings for children with ASD are still a decision that many schools and families wrestle with. Parents and teachers must carefully weigh many factors to make individual decisions about the right placement for a particular child at that time.

8 Visual and Hearing Impairments

We rely on our five senses to take in and interpret information about the world. A disorder affecting one or more of the senses can significantly impact a child's ability to learn and to interact with others and his environment. Disabilities that involve vision or hearing are uncommon and considered low-incidence disabilities. Generally, several professionals work together to design the individualized interventions a child needs, and although there is a range of educational settings for children with sensory impairments, many are successfully included in general education settings.

Visual Impairments: Blindness and Low Vision

Tirzah was born with no useful vision, but that has never slowed her down. Now in second grade, she loves to be part of the classroom lessons, especially when Mrs. Freeman reads wonderful books out loud and everyone talks about them. Tirzah has always enjoyed science, too—until this year. Last year her teacher had the students do lots of hands-on experiments. Tirzah could hold the materials and feel the changes that occurred, and she relished these activities.

Mrs. Freeman does not do experiments like this. Most of the time, the students just watch her do the experiments and then they draw pictures of what happened. Tirzah feels left out. She does not know what is happening during the experiments until Mrs. Freeman tells her. Instead of drawing a picture, Tirzah types out her answers on a worksheet. When she asks the teacher if there are some experiments she could be a part of, Mrs. Freeman says that she is sorry, but the experiments aren't safe for a child who is blind. This makes Tirzah very upset.

Tirzah's mom, wanting her daughter to be more included in valuable science instruction, meets with the district's science supervisor, Mr. Antonakis, to see if the school can find ways to have Tirzah participate more actively. Mr. Antonakis does some research and finds the Perkins School for the Blind's website, which offers accessible science activities and dozens of ideas on how to make science come alive. Together, he, Mrs. Freeman, and the teacher of the visually impaired who works with Tirzah a few times each week review the types of experiments that Tirzah and the rest of the students could all participate in. With some coaching from the teacher of the visually impaired, Mrs. Freeman begins to feel comfortable with helping Tirzah be more actively involved.

Vision helps children understand and learn about the environment they live in, the people they interact with, and the language they hear. Because so much of learning in the early years occurs visually, a child with impaired vision requires modifications and adaptations to both the environment and instruction to learn at the same pace as her peers.

What Are Visual Impairments?

The term *visual impairment* is broad and describes the effects of various eye disorders. The eyes and the brain work together to help an individual see, and if parts of the eyes are damaged or not working correctly, or the eyes and the brain do not communicate properly, vision may be impaired. A child with a visual impairment may have partial vision or none at all.

According to the National Eye Institute (NEI 2017), the most common vision problems are refractive errors, in which the shape of the eye interferes with the ability to focus. These errors can result in such common conditions as nearsightedness, farsightedness, astigmatism, and presbyopia. Refractive errors are usually correctable with eyeglasses, contact lenses, or surgery. Other, more serious conditions may involve the eye muscles, blood vessels in the eyes, or damage in an area of the brain necessary for proper sight.

Vision impairments can result in a child having low vision, which means a visual acuity of 20/70 or worse (20/20 is considered perfect vision) that cannot be corrected (Kellogg Eye Center 2017). For example, a child may see only light, shadows, and indistinct shapes. Legal blindness refers to an acuity of 20/200. Most children with a visual impairment have some useful vision; only a small percentage of individuals experience total blindness.

Possible Reasons for Visual Impairments

Children may be born with impaired sight or lose vision later on. Hereditary conditions, diseases, illnesses, neurological conditions, and accidents can all cause loss of vision in children.

A Closer Look at Some Causes of Visual Impairments

In addition to refractive vision problems, other conditions can impact young children's vision and impede their learning. These include **strabismus,** a condition in which the muscles surrounding the eyes prevent both eyes from being able to look at the same thing at the same time, significantly affecting a child's depth perception (Donahue et al. 2014). **Retinopathy of prematurity** is a disease that impacts the blood vessels in the eye and occurs in some premature babies who received oxygen therapy to develop their lungs while in neonatal intensive care. It can lead to permanent blindness (AAPOS 2016).

Cortical visual impairment (CVI) is caused by a problem in the brain with processing what the eye sees, rather than a problem in the eye itself. Children with CVI may have difficulty attending to visual stimuli, delayed responses to what they see, and/or better vision when they look at objects that are moving (or appear to be, like sparkly objects). The condition does not generally lead to total blindness. CVI can happen from an injury at birth, including a lack of oxygen in the blood or a lack of blood to the brain. Traumatic brain injuries, strokes, and infections of the central nervous system such as meningitis and encephalitis can also cause CVI (Roman-Lantzy 2007).

Impact of Visual Impairments on Development and Learning

Having a visual disorder affects a wide range of skills—navigating the environment, detecting and avoiding hazards, performing daily activities, relating to other people, and learning language, concepts, and what the world is like. Limited vision affects a child's ability to fully experience the world and build concrete knowledge, and since children learn many self-help skills through observation, a child with impaired vision may experience delays in learning skills like eating, dressing, and personal hygiene.

Visual impairments also impact social development. Limited vision affects a child's ability to understand nonverbal clues, such as when it is his turn to talk. Without eye contact, a child may appear disinterested in a conversation, which affects his ability to sustain interactions with other people.

Many children with visual impairments do not have learning disabilities or other disabilities in addition to their vision impairment. Many learn the same academic skills as their sighted peers, but they learn them in adapted ways. Some children are able to use what vision they have to learn, perhaps aided by magnifiers, while others rely on their other senses as well as additional aids such as technology.

Children with vision impairments need specific interventions. Being included in the classroom with their peers is very common, and ideally every child with a visual disability will have the assistance of a trained teacher of the visually impaired who visits the classroom to help the teacher adapt and modify activities and the environment and understand the tools the child is using. This professional often provides some direct instruction to the child as well.

Identifying Visual Impairments

These signs may indicate that a child is having difficulty seeing (AAP 2016; NCBDDD 2017; The Vision Council 2017):

- » Squinting
- » Closing or covering one eye to look at something
- » Holding objects close to her face, like books or screens
- » Frequently tilting his head to one side
- » Rubbing her eyes repeatedly
- » Experiencing redness or tearing in one or both eyes
- » Blinking excessively
- » Being sensitive to light
- » Complaining of blurriness or being out of sorts when looking at things closely for a period of time
- » Having eyes that look crossed, turn out or in, don't focus together, flutter, or are watery

In babies older than 4 months, adults should watch for difficulty tracking objects across the line of sight or inability to make steady eye contact (Kirkendoll 2016). Drifting or crossed eyes beyond this age also may indicate a visual impairment. All children should have their vision checked early—as a newborn and at well-baby visits. In addition, if parents or teachers suspect a child may not be seeing properly, a visit to a pediatric ophthalmologist should be scheduled. Detecting a problem early increases the chances of correction and helps to avoid further issues, and early intervention for more serious problems is vital.

Strategies for the Classroom

Each state has an agency that assists families and schools in identifying the educational services each child needs, including a teacher of the visually impaired. This professional works with children on specific vision-related skills (AFB 2017a; AFB 2017b):

- » **Orientation and mobility (O&M) skills.** Children with vision impairments need to learn how to get around different (and unknown) environments safely and independently.
- » **Assistive technology skills.** Many children with visual impairments need to access computers through means other than a mouse or touchpad. Assistive technologies like braille-adapted keyboards enable children to use computers independently. Voice recognition software and screen readers—software that converts text displayed on a computer screen to speech or a braille display—are commonly used by individuals with vision impairments.
- » **Braille.** Children with significant vision impairments learn to read and write using **braille,** a system of raised dots that are read with the fingers.

In addition to specific skills addressed by the teacher of the visually impaired, everyday adaptations and modifications can support children with visual impairments in the classroom.

Encourage Independence

» Watch for well-meaning adults and peers who seem overprotective of a child with impaired vision or who join the child for activities or social situations because they want to "help" her. Keep a watchful eye on the child with a visual impairment, but avoid offering more assistance than she needs during classroom activities and play. Resist the urge to do things for her because you fear it will be too difficult or take too long.

» Let the child explore the environment and navigate to the places he wants to go. Do not always have someone else lead him. This is especially important as the child gets older and starts to use new tools for mobility, such as a cane or a guide dog.

» Keep the environment clean and organized. Provide enough room for the child to navigate, and make sure materials are easy to locate.

» Have high expectations for a child with a visual impairment, just as you would for any child. Do not treat her differently or ignore challenging behavior.

» Facilitate friendships between a child with a visual impairment and his peers. Partner children for activities. Children without disabilities take their cues from you on how to act toward a child with a disability. If you are accepting, they will be too.

» Teach an older child how to navigate a new environment before school starts or during times when other students are not there.

Modify the Environment

» Look at the labels in your environment. Add something tactile in addition to print and braille. For example, have a special texture such as sandpaper on the labels to indicate that these are materials the child can handle, and use a contrasting texture, like a smooth and silky fabric, to indicate the location of materials that are to be used only by the teacher. Be sure the child learns what these tactile cues mean.

» Provide objects that are brightly colored or on high-contrast backgrounds.

» Provide dress-up materials that are easy for a child with a vision disability to manipulate. For clothing that has small hooks and eyes, add other ways to fasten them, such as Velcro.

» Add textures to finger paints, and put the child's paper on a tray with sides or inside a shirt box so he can feel the boundaries.

» Use textures to create letters, numbers, and words the child can trace and feel. Use glue or cut the shapes from sponge or felt.

» Keep in mind that real objects are always better than plastic replicas. Offer real materials that relate to the content children are learning and that they can touch, smell, feel, and taste. For younger children, provide food containers for dramatic play that are the real size and weight instead of plastic so that they can touch and explore. Provide collections of natural objects, such as shells and bird nests.

» Have braille books and story props along with picture books.

» Encourage art exploration. Include many 3-D art materials like foam, cotton balls, and wood scraps for the child to create with.

» Make sure the environment in the primary grade classroom includes signage with braille. A child should learn to read the signs in the environment from an early age.

Modify Activities and Lessons

» When you present something visually, use an object the child with a visual impairment can touch and manipulate or that produces a sound that brings meaning to the activity. If you are demonstrating something, try to position yourself near the child so she can better see and hear what you are doing.

» Verbalize everything. Use all children's names rather than just nodding at or pointing to them. Whatever you write on a chart or a child's paper, verbalize as you write it. Remember the universal design principles discussed in Chapter 3? This strategy is a good example—it benefits all children.

» Use clear directions. Phrases like "over here" are confusing to a child with a vision disability.

» Make activities and lessons active. Instead of learning about the farm only through books and videos, take the class to a farm to experience the animals and planting or harvesting techniques. Again, all children benefit from these hands-on, minds-on experiences.

» Give the child extra time to explore materials and to complete and practice lessons, particularly when he is learning something new or still learning a technique, like using a braille writer. With time and proper support, most children with visual impairments will eventually be able to keep to the same pace as other children.

» As the child gets older, make sure as much of her work as possible is done using braille technology. Braille readers and writers can be used with children starting in the primary grades. A teacher of the visually impaired will teach braille, but every teacher can make sure the child uses it each day.

Visual Impairments Summary

While many children with visual impairments can learn academic skills along with their sighted peers, they need adaptations to do so. They also require specific interventions to learn how to move around safely and independently, effectively use the vision they have, and use assistive technologies.

Hearing Impairments

Everyone agrees that Cèsar is such an easy baby. At 2 months old, he sleeps right through the dog barking at the mail carrier and his two siblings running and yelling while they play. While his mother, Eva, is happy that Cèsar is calm most of the day, she has a very hard time soothing him when he is fussy. He doesn't seem to respond to her whispers in his ears or to the musical mobile in his room that his siblings had loved. Nothing seems to pacify him.

Eva is about to go back to work full-time, and she hopes the child care center that Cèsar's siblings attended will help her figure out how to soothe him. The caregivers there are the best at figuring out what works and what doesn't for babies. They helped Eva so much with her other children when they were young.

Cèsar's caregiver, Anna, starts to notice some things about his development. He isn't starting to "talk" (making vowel sounds like *oh* and *ah*) yet when she plays with him, and he doesn't seem to react to familiar voices in the classroom.

Anna talks to Eva about her concerns and suggests that she have the pediatrician check Cèsar's hearing at the next visit. At the doctor's office, Eva is shocked to learn that Cèsar has significant hearing loss in both ears. At the pediatrician's recommendation, she takes her son to an audiologist who specializes in treating infants with hearing loss, and Cèsar is fitted with hearing aids. It takes a long time for him to get used to these, and he often tries to pull them out like some babies yank off hats or socks. The early interventionist who has begun to work with the family advises both Eva and Anna to start by putting the hearing aids in only during times Cèsar has direct interaction with them, and then take them out for a while. As Cèsar slowly adjusts to all of the new sounds he is hearing, he seems to really enjoy anything that makes noise, including rattles, bells, and his mom's voice.

Because language, speech, and hearing are all interconnected, identifying hearing loss early is important. Speech and language skills develop rapidly before the age of 3, and when a hearing loss is not identified, children will be delayed in developing these skills (March of Dimes 2014a). The CDC recommends that every newborn be screened for hearing loss as early as possible, usually before they leave the hospital (2015c). Professionals such as audiologists, speech-language therapists, and sign language specialists work closely with teachers to maximize a child's hearing, communication, and learning.

What Are Hearing Impairments?

A hearing impairment is a partial or total inability to hear. The CDC (2015c) uses the term *hearing loss* to describe any degree of hearing impairment, including deafness. IDEA defines *hearing impairment* and *deafness* as separate terms and eligibility categories.

Hearing impairments range from mild, where a person might hear some sounds but have difficulty differentiating speech in noisy environments, to profound. Individuals with profound hearing loss may be able to detect and feel the vibrations of some very loud sounds, but they cannot hear any speech. A hearing impairment to this degree is considered deafness. Depending on the type of damage, hearing loss may be temporary or permanent. Some types of hearing loss can be treated with surgery, medicine, or through the use of a hearing aid; other types are not helped by hearing aids (CDC 2015c).

Possible Reasons for Hearing Impairments

A hearing impairment may be congenital (present at birth) or acquired later due to obstruction, damage, illness, or disease in the outer, middle, or inner part of the ear.

Congenital loss can be caused by

- » Infections or other complications during pregnancy (maternal diabetes, rhesus [Rh] factor)
- » Premature birth
- » Family history of deafness or hearing loss
- » Another disability (such as Down syndrome)

Acquired causes of hearing loss include

- » Ear infections
- » Fluid behind the eardrum
- » Head injuries
- » Childhood illnesses (measles, mumps, chicken pox)
- » Repeated exposure to loud noises (ASHA 2017a)

Impact of Hearing Impairments on Development and Learning

Although many children with hearing impairments do have not additional disabilities, most are eligible for special education under IDEA because the impairment is likely to impact the child's ability to comprehend verbal language and thus his educational performance. Learning vocabulary, word order, grammar, and other aspects of language is more difficult for children with hearing impairments.

While a hearing impairment does not impact a child's overall intellectual capacity, it may affect her academically, socially, and emotionally. A young child with even a mild impairment may have difficulty hearing what others are saying, understanding how speech is moderated, learning new words, and saying words correctly. A child's speech may be difficult for others to understand. If conversation is too frustrating for a child to follow and participate in, she may avoid social interactions with other children, which can lead to the child feeling isolated.

Identifying Hearing Impairments

Although infants typically have a hearing screen early, it's still important to look for signs that a baby or young child may not be hearing properly. If an infant isn't startled by loud

sounds, doesn't turn his head when he hears a sound or his name being called, appears to hear some sounds but not others, or doesn't say single words by the age of 1, he may have a hearing loss (CDC 2015c).

These signs may indicate hearing loss in young children:

» Doesn't respond consistently to sounds or her own name

» Asks for things to be repeated or often says "huh?"

» Is delayed in developing speech or has unclear speech

» Turns the volume up loud on the TV and other electronic devices

» Doesn't follow directions (CDC 2015c)

It's vital to follow up with a physician if hearing loss is suspected. If a child fails a hearing screening, the doctor should refer the child for an evaluation by an audiologist, a professional trained to test hearing. The audiologist uses a variety of tests to determine whether the child has a hearing loss and, if so, what type and to what degree.

Addressing Hearing Impairments

Two important factors to consider in supporting a child's hearing and language development are hearing technologies and communication approaches.

Hearing Technologies

Children with hearing impairments may benefit from assistive hearing technologies. Assistive devices cannot replace a child's natural hearing, but they are tools that can help the child hear better and be able to enjoy, respond to, and interact with her environment.

Hearing aids are one of the most commonly used technology devices to help with hearing loss. Young children typically use behind-the-ear (BTE) hearing aids. As a child grows,

Deaf or deaf

People in the Deaf community differentiate between these two terms:

- *deaf* identifies the medical condition of being unable to hear
- *Deaf* identifies the group of people who share the same language—sign—and culture

While many people outside of the Deaf community may not understand this difference, it is important to appreciate that members of the Deaf community do not view deafness as a disability or a condition that needs to be fixed. It is part of their human experience (Padden & Humphries 2006). Members of the Deaf community share a language and culture that is rich in history and traditions across many generations, and Deaf culture needs to be respected in the same ways that other cultures are respected.

Members of the Deaf community take pride in their identity and reject people-first language (e.g., *a person who is deaf, a person who is hard of hearing*), preferring identity-first language—*a Deaf person* or *a hard-of-hearing person* (Lum 2011).

the device may have to be changed and adjusted. An audiologist can explain what the hearing aid is able and not able to do for a specific child. The audiologist can also program the hearing aid so it can be adjusted for different environments, such as classrooms and outdoor play areas (NIDCD 2017b).

Cochlear implants are a relatively newer option for young children with more profound hearing loss. Instead of amplifying sounds as hearing aids do, a cochlear implant directly stimulates the auditory nerve. It does not cure deafness or restore normal hearing, but it does help an individual understand some speech and sounds in the environment (NIDCD 2017a). If introduced when the child is very young, cochlear implants can make a dramatic difference in hearing.

Frequency-modulated (FM) systems help reduce background noise, improve the clearness of speech, and improve hearing when the speaker is farther away. A microphone is worn on the teacher's (or other speaker's) lapel or as a headset or placed on a tabletop. The microphone then transmits radio waves into a receiver that is built into the child's hearing aid or cochlear implant, worn on the child's body, or placed in the room.

Communication Approaches

Being able to communicate with others, ask questions, and make their wants and needs known is an essential part of development for all children. A child with impaired hearing might use speech, sign language, or a combination to communicate; some children use augmentative communication devices. There are varying viewpoints on the best approach, and this decision must be made by a family together with their physician and other professionals based on the child and family's needs and situation.

Speech. Some children with mild or moderate hearing loss learn to use what hearing they have to develop speech. If a hearing impairment is diagnosed early and intervention begins right away, extensive speech therapy or a combination of speech therapy and hearing technologies enables some children to develop speech that is understood by others. Oral language allows children to communicate more easily with hearing individuals.

While some children with mild or moderate hearing loss are able to develop speech, not all do. The ability to hear and discriminate sounds and then reproduce those sounds so that someone else understands them is complex, and many children with more severe hearing impairments are not able to master these skills.

Sign language. A manual communication method, sign language is made up of a system of gestures made with a person's hands, arms, and body (Stokoe, Casterline, & Croneberg 1965). Sign language is not a single, universal language spoken by Deaf people around the world; each country and region has its own dialect. American Sign Language (ASL) is its own language with its own rules for grammar and syntax. It has almost nothing grammatically in common with spoken English.

Research suggests that all young children who are hearing impaired, even those who have or will receive cochlear implants, benefit from learning sign language as early as possible (Mellon et al. 2015). Pediatricians may advise families to consider the addition of sign language rather than rely solely on using spoken language with their child.

Some students who use sign language will have a sign language interpreter in school with them to help them communicate. This individual is there to interpret for the child, not as a support to the teacher.

Using a combination of methods. Many children communicate using a combination of listening, lip reading, facial expressions, gesturing, signing, and speaking. Known as **total communication**, the idea is that a child uses whatever methods work best for her.

Some hearing families of young children with hearing loss use a combination of sign language and spoken English known as Manually Coded English (MCE), which uses the same signs of ASL but more closely follows the grammar, word order, and sentence structure of spoken English (Schick 2011).

Augmentative communication devices. Children can also use assistive technology to communicate. Augmentative communication devices, or software on a smartphone or tablet, can be used to generate speech. For example, a child touches a picture or photo to have prerecorded words said aloud. As children get older, this technology can be used in more sophisticated ways; the same kinds of devices have an unlimited vocabulary and can read typed words aloud.

A physical disability may affect a child's ability to use his legs, his upper body, or both; he may have more difficulty using one side of his body than the other. Some children walk unaided, while others may have leg braces or use a wheelchair or walker some or all of the time. Many, like Jayla, require rather simple accommodations and modifications—and a little imagination on the part of teachers—to be fully included with children without disabilities. Others need an array of supports from different professionals to move, communicate, socialize, and learn. Understanding individual children's strengths and needs and providing appropriate supports and therapies will enable children to actively participate to the greatest extent possible in the early childhood setting.

What Are Physical Disabilities?

Children with a physical disability have a medical condition that significantly impacts their ability to move from place to place, move specific parts of their body, and sustain energy. Several medical conditions can result in physical disabilities, including the following:

» **Cerebral palsy:** Also known as CP, cerebral palsy is one of the most common physical disabilities in childhood (Accardo 2007). It is not one specific disease or disability; the term indicates injury or damage to parts of the brain that control a person's muscles. Injury can occur during pregnancy, delivery, or soon after birth. CP is discussed in more detail later in this chapter.

» **Spina bifida:** The term *spina bifida* means "open spine" and is a condition that occurs during prenatal development. The child's developing spine fails to close all the way, and a sac of fluid—sometimes containing part of the spinal cord—may bulge through the opening. This can cause moderate to severe loss of feeling in the child's lower half of the body, affecting her ability to walk and control bladder functions (March of Dimes 2014b). A child with spina bifida may also have hydrocephalus, a condition caused by excess fluid building up in the brain and causing pressure.

» **Spinal cord injuries:** Complete or partial spinal cord injuries may occur during the birthing process or in an accident after birth. Complete spinal cord injuries paralyze a child from the spot of injury and down the rest of the body. Partial spinal cord injuries will leave the child with some feeling and some movement from the spot of the injury and down the rest of the body (Hayes & Arriola 2005).

» **Traumatic brain injuries:** Traumatic brain injury (TBI) refers to damage to the brain caused by a child's head hitting something very hard (like the ground, or a bat or ball when playing), or the child's head being shaken violently, such as during a car accident or incident of physical abuse (shaken baby syndrome). The physical effects of TBI include paralysis, difficulty with balance and motor coordination, and stiffness or tightness of muscles used for movement and speech (BIAA 2017). Children may also have difficulty with memory, attention, reasoning, and other areas that impact learning and everyday functioning.

» **Muscular dystrophy:** A genetic disorder, muscular dystrophy weakens a child's muscles over time. As the condition progresses, more muscles are affected, including those of the heart and respiratory system (MDA 2017).

and actively participate with other children? The IEP team, including the child's parents, teachers, and program administrator, must consult with the child's physical therapist and other professionals to determine whether any major changes to the physical environment are necessary and achievable.

Promoting Independence in the Environment

» Make sure that the floor is free of any hazards and barriers. If you do have area rugs, make sure they are secure and won't cause a child to trip.

» Use furniture that is heavy and stable so nothing can be knocked over easily or unintentionally.

» Position furniture so that a child using a walker or a wheelchair can navigate the room independently.

» Make sure all seating arrangements are appropriate, comfortable, and safe for the child. Work with parents and/or the child's physical therapist to plan for having the child sit in many different places—at the table, on the floor, and on outdoor play equipment.

» Make materials accessible and portable. If it is not possible to have some materials accessible at all times to a child with a physical disability, keep them in a clear container so they are visible and all children know they can use them. Set materials in a variety of places throughout the room where the child with a disability and his peers can play and work together.

» Have a place for any equipment (wheelchair, walker, crutches) the child uses for part of the day to be stored out of the way so they are safe but near enough to be accessible whenever the child needs them.

» Organize self-care activities so the child can be independent. If the children use cubbies, assign the child with a disability one on the end of the row so she has ample room to take care of her possessions by herself.

» Provide stabilization bars or other equipment in the bathroom so the child can take care of his toileting and handwashing needs as independently as possible. If the child cannot be independent with toileting, make sure a plan is in place that takes age-appropriate modesty into consideration and treats the child with dignity.

Cerebral Palsy

Cerebral palsy (CP) is a group of disorders that affects posture and balance, muscle control and coordination (including speech and chewing), and even reflexes such as swallowing. It results from an injury to or lack of development in the area of the brain that controls movement of muscles. Cerebral palsy is not progressive. It is more common among boys than girls.

The effects of CP can be mild, moderate, or severe, ranging from having a somewhat clumsy gait to using a wheelchair or other special equipment all of the time. The extent of the injury to the part of the brain that controls the muscles determines how severe the CP will be. The more severe the CP, the more likely it is that a child will also have intellectual, language, visual, and/or hearing disabilities (ADDM CP Network 2013).

Types of Cerebral Palsy

Cerebral palsy is sometimes described based on where and to what extent parts of the body are impacted. Children with CP may be affected in only one limb (monoplegia), in the arm and leg on one side of the body (hemiplegia), in both legs (paraplegia), or in all four limbs (quadriplegia) (Pakula, Van Naarden Braun, & Yeargin-Allsopp 2009).

Cerebral palsy is also described by the way it affects a person's movements (ADDM CP Network 2013). The most common type, known as spastic CP, causes stiff, jerky movements, making it very difficult or almost impossible for a person to be able to move in certain ways at will. This type impacts about 70–80 percent of all people with cerebral palsy. Athetoid, or dyskinetic, CP happens when the signal from the brain to the spinal cord is misinterpreted, and it is characterized by involuntary, uncontrollable movements. This makes it difficult for the child to walk or control a part of his body the way he wants to. Individuals with ataxic CP have balance and coordination problems that make their movements look unsteady or clumsy.

Facts About Cerebral Palsy

- More than half (58 percent) of children identified with CP can walk independently.
- Many children with CP also have at least one other condition, such as epilepsy, intellectual disabilities, or ASD.
- The rate of children born with CP has stayed relatively stable over the past 50 years, even as the number of babies born at risk for CP (because of conditions like premature birth or low birth weight) has dramatically increased.
- The number of children with CP who also have moderate to severe intellectual disabilities has decreased about 2.6 percent each year from 1985 to 2002. This suggests that improved medical care for mothers during pregnancy and for infants may be preventing more significant forms of CP. (Van Naarden Braun et al. 2016)

» Adaptive equipment needs repair or replacing from time to time. Keep an eye out for malfunctions and address them right away with the child's therapist or family.

» Make sure the child with a physical disability is on the same visual level as everyone else throughout as much of the day as possible. If she must remain in her wheelchair during large group time, consider having everyone else sit in chairs instead of on the floor.

» Because a physical disability is visible, many peers are curious and want to know about it. Set up your class library with books that teach about the disability itself or show a character with the same disability.

Promoting Independence During Activities and Lessons

» Hands-on learning experiences are important for all children, so make sure that the child with a physical disability has lots of opportunities to participate, even if he needs assistance. Let him do as much as he can, as independently as he can.

» Keep objects steady when a child is using them. If she is painting, stabilize the paper and the paint by taping the paper to the table or placing the paper on a no-skid surface or inside a shirt box.

» Provide choices for what the child can do or how he can participate. A sense of autonomy is important, and feeling that he can make things happen gives him a sense of accomplishment and control and makes an activity more meaningful.

» Give children enough time to explore, create, and discover. To actively participate in all activities, children whose movements are limited or difficult must know they have enough time. Older children may need additional time to complete assignments and tests.

» Remember that a child with a physical disability may tire more easily when participating in activities that require exertion. Alternate times when the child needs to be active with more restful activities, like reading a book with an adult.

» Make sure everything a child needs is within reach. Put puzzles and small manipulatives on a tray with sides or inside a shirt box so they are easy to reach and will not get lost.

» Provide materials and instructions in different formats and at different levels of difficulty. For a child who needs to work on using both hands together, offer toys that require the use of two hands. Have different types of blocks, some that connect easily and others that require more complex balancing skills.

» Use virtual materials and manipulatives on a computer that are easier to use than real objects.

» Use assistive technology so a child can complete her classwork as independently as possible, such as by typing or completing classwork on a computer that is specially designed for her.

» Work for success. Even if a child cannot be independent in all parts of an activity, he can do something by himself. Structure activities to provide some aspect of independence and success, even if for one small part of a task. Encourage him to try, even when activities are difficult.

» If a child has difficulty physically raising her hand in class to let the teacher know she has something to contribute, work together to find an alternative, like pressing a buzzer.

» If pencil and paper tasks are too difficult, consider having the child give a combination of written and oral responses.

Promoting Independence with Peers

» Brainstorm with the children ways they could include their classmate with a physical disability in their play activities.

» Answer children's questions about a peer's disability honestly and positively. Encourage the child with a disability to answer these questions as well, if she is comfortable doing so.

» Children with physical disabilities may have frequent absences for medical appointments, illness, and so on. Talk with the other children to explain and allay any fears that something might be seriously wrong with the child.

» Model how to respect a child's personal space and boundaries. Teach peers not to crowd around a child with a physical disability or relegate him to the back of a group activity where he can't readily participate.

» Teach peers to never push a child's wheelchair. Moving a child's wheelchair from place to place is always the job of the child herself or an adult.

» Teach children to ask the child with a physical disability if he wants help before doing something for him. Also, teach the child with a physical disability to identify his own boundaries and to respectfully tell others when he does not need help.

» Encourage all children to celebrate when anyone accomplishes something new on their own.

» Work with community agencies to adapt recreation and sports facilities to make them more inclusive of people with physical disabilities. When children with physical disabilities can participate in and enjoy the same activities and places as their peers, they are more likely to be included and accepted.

Summary

Physical disabilities can limit what a child can do, but it does not have to stop her from participating in high-quality programs and learning alongside her peers. Along with therapies and assistive technologies where appropriate, provide an environment where children learn to be as independent as possible.

10 Intellectual Disabilities

Maggie, an engaging 3½-year-old with Down syndrome, is enrolled in Ms. Ellie's class at a child care center in a synagogue in Maggie's community. When Maggie starts school, Ms. Ellie is told by her director that the public school district's speech-language therapist, Tamaira, and the occupational therapist, Paolo, will visit regularly to work with Maggie as well as support Ms. Ellie.

The first few days, Maggie wants to be held most of the day. After a week or so, Ms. Ellie realizes that Maggie continues to need a lot of attention. She clings to Ms. Ellie and won't talk to her classmates. Tamaira and Paolo come a few days every week to work with Maggie and offer suggestions on how to help her in the classroom. Although she listens to their advice, Ms. Ellie is just grateful to have someone else there to give some attention to Maggie, even for just a few minutes.

Maggie gradually starts to interact with the other children, but she does not seem to know how to play appropriately. She often knocks down the other children's block structures or grabs toys from their hands. When center time is over, she sometimes refuses to go to the rug for group time, instead going to the art table and throwing markers and crayons on the floor or running to hide in the reading center. By the end of Maggie's third month in the classroom, no one wants to play with her.

Ms. Ellie begins to think that her classroom is not the right classroom for Maggie, that maybe she should be in a class with other preschoolers who have disabilities where she can be taught by a special education teacher with specialized training and knowledge. Ms. Ellie decides to meet with the therapists to discuss her concerns.

Tamaira and Paolo do not see the situation the same way. They tell Ms. Ellie that Maggie is making progress—slowly, but it *is* progress. Maggie is using a few more words than when she started in the program, and even Ms. Ellie admits that she doesn't put toys in her mouth as often now, something Paolo has been working on. The therapists offer suggestions to help Maggie be more independent in the classroom routines and activities and play appropriately.

Because Maggie's challenging behavior often occurs during transition times, Tamaira makes a large picture schedule and posts it for the whole class so they can easily see what activity is next. Maggie adjusts to everyone looking at the schedule after every part of the day, and it makes transitions easier for her. Tamaira and Paolo also make it a priority to support and teach Ms. Ellie how to work with Maggie on the days they don't come to school. One of the things Tamaira models for her is narrating Maggie's play, an important part of fostering language skills and concepts.

When they meet again, Ms. Ellie admits that Maggie is making some progress. She still doesn't talk much or play with the other children, but she is becoming more independent. Maggie is also starting to pretend more. She loves feeding and rocking the dolls, and although her speech is often hard to understand, she is starting to talk about what she is doing. Tamaira is thrilled with this progress, but Ms. Ellie still thinks this may not be the best place for Maggie. There are plenty of other issues to address.

Not long after, Ms. Ellie notices that Maggie and another girl in her class, Violet, are becoming friends. They sit next to one another at group time, play with the dolls together, and sometimes even hold hands while walking to the playground. This is the moment Ms. Ellie knows that her classroom is the right one for Maggie after all.

Young children with intellectual disabilities, like Maggie, face a variety of challenges over their lifetime. The more the adults in a child's life understand how the intellectual disability impacts her, how to support her in day-to-day activities, and how to create opportunities for success, the better they can help her overcome many of those challenges. Creating opportunities for success, encouraging independence, and fostering friendships can make an enormous difference in the life of a child with an intellectual disability.

What's in a name? Plenty

Rosa's Law (Public Law 111-256) is a US federal law signed by former President Barack Obama in 2010 that removes the terms *mental retardation* and *mentally retarded* from federal health, education, and labor policies and replaces them with people-first language—*intellectual disability* and *individual with an intellectual disability*. The law is named for Rosa Marcellino, a young girl with Down syndrome who, along with her parents and siblings, fought to have the law changed first in her home state of Maryland and then in the whole country. The intention of the law is to highlight the fact that words do matter and to help change the perceptions society has of individuals with intellectual disabilities.

What Are Intellectual Disabilities?

A person who has an intellectual disability has lifelong impaired intellectual functioning, meaning an intelligence quotient (IQ) that is below average, as well as difficulty with adaptive functioning—self-help and decision-making skills that are needed to live independently (APA 2013). These characteristics make it difficult to learn new concepts and skills. A 4-year-old with an intellectual disability might appear to be more similar in development to a 2-year-old child without a disability.

Possible Reasons for Intellectual Disabilities

About 25 to 50 percent of intellectual disabilities are due to genetic causes, such as a full or partial extra chromosome (such as Down syndrome), a defective chromosome (Williams syndrome), or an inherited chromosomal disorder (such as fragile X syndrome) (CNDD 2012; Kaufman, Ayub, & Vincent 2010).

In some children, an intellectual disability is linked to exposure to a toxic substance like drugs or alcohol during pregnancy or a lack of oxygen during birth (CNDD 2012). Children can also be at risk from certain illnesses (measles, meningitis, whooping cough, and seizure disorders), injuries (head injuries and near-drowning experiences), or exposure to toxic substances (lead in contaminated water, paint, or soil) when they are very young (ASHA 2017d; Center for Parent Information and Resources 2015). In many cases, the cause of a child's intellectual disability is unknown.

Impact of Intellectual Disabilities on Development and Learning

There is a wide range of intellectual disabilities. As with many other delays and disabilities, children are affected differently. With a mild intellectual disability, children need concrete, direct instruction in skills such as planning, reasoning, problem solving, and generalizing what they learn to new situations (APA 2013). However, they can learn academic and social skills that help them successfully engage in many school and community activities with little or no support.

Lead and intellectual disabilities

There is strong evidence that children can develop an intellectual disability when they are exposed to lead in their environments over an extended period of time, from a few months to a few years (ACCLPP 2012). Exposure can occur from dust from lead paint or water from contaminated lead pipes. Lead is found in contaminated soil, some pottery, and even older toys made in certain parts of the world. When the body absorbs lead, the brain and nervous system do not develop normally. Lead poisoning is very serious and can even be fatal for very young children (ACCLPP 2012; WHO 2010). Symptoms of lead poisoning include developmental delays, irritability, loss of appetite, fatigue, eating nonfood items, and seizures (Mayo Clinic 2016b).

Children with moderate intellectual disabilities have more noticeable problems with speech and motor skills. They can still communicate in simple ways, dress themselves, and take care of their basic self-care needs (bathing, toileting), but they may always need some support or supervision (APA 2013).

Children with severe intellectual disabilities may take longer to learn to walk, talk, dress, and eat by themselves, and those most severely affected require lifelong supervision. Some of these children also have physical disabilities. A very small number of children have profound intellectual disabilities that require them to be completely dependent on others for 24-hour care and support (APA 2013).

Children with intellectual disabilities can and will learn. They may take longer to learn concepts and skills than other children, and more abstract concepts may be beyond their reach, but every child will be able to learn some of the skills they need.

Identifying Intellectual Disabilities

Signs of severe and profound intellectual disabilities often appear during infancy and toddlerhood and are more pronounced than signs of a mild or moderate intellectual disability. Children with mild intellectual disabilities may not be diagnosed until the primary grades, when academic demands start to increase and they have more difficulty keeping up with their peers. Children with severe and profound intellectual disabilities are more likely to have an additional diagnosis, such as cerebral palsy.

Young children with an intellectual disability may show characteristics such as

- » Poor muscle tone (sometimes called "floppy")
- » Difficulty with nursing or bottle feeding, either with a weak ability to suck or difficulty coordinating swallowing while feeding
- » Lack of interest in other people or pets, or a lack of recognition of familiar caregivers
- » Lack of babbling or repeating of sounds
- » Delay in developing motor skills, such as rolling over, sitting up, crawling, and walking
- » Delay in developing language skills; may talk late or have trouble with talking
- » Delay in mastering self-help (adaptive) skills like dressing, feeding themselves, and toileting
- » Difficulty understanding and following social rules
- » Trouble seeing the consequences of what they do
- » Difficulty with problem solving and reasoning logically (AAP 2015; ASHA 2017d)

The determination of an intellectual disability is based on two criteria: the results of an IQ test and observations of a child's adaptive functioning. An IQ test is administered by a professional, usually a licensed psychologist. The average IQ score is 100, and most people score between 85 and 115. A score of less than 70 indicates that a child may have an intellectual disability (Hunt 2011).

The second part of determining whether a child has an intellectual disability—adaptive functioning—is also important. When evaluating for adaptive functioning skills, a doctor will observe the child directly as well as ask parents how well their child communicates and interacts in social situations with different people and takes care of her own needs, like feeding and dressing. If the child's IQ score is below average and a doctor finds her adaptive functioning to also be impaired, the child is considered to have an intellectual disability (Center for Parent Information and Resources 2015).

Strategies for the Classroom

Each child who has an intellectual disability possesses unique strengths, needs, personality traits, and preferences outside of his disability. A child's behavior—such as being cranky after sitting in a group for a long time—may not necessarily be due to a limited understanding of expectations or an inability to regulate his emotions. He may simply be tired after a period of concentration and need to be allowed to rest or do something by himself.

While it is important that children with intellectual disabilities have access to the same programs and are held to the same learning standards as every other child, some also need direct instruction in the basic skills they need to be self-sufficient in adulthood—dressing, eating, walking, talking, socializing and interacting in their community, working in some capacity, and so on. They may need additional instruction for a longer period of time than other children. Together, the IEP team members determine what supports a child needs to be successful in school, at home, and in the community.

Teaching basic skills may occur in small groups or one-to-one in the classroom, or outside of the classroom. Some children with intellectual disabilities may need more specialized teaching from a special education teacher or other specialist to learn communication skills (talking and making their wants and needs known), personal care needs (dressing, eating, and toileting), health and safety (handwashing), and social skills (following routines, sharing and cooperating, and resolving conflicts).

Teaching Specific Skills

Hands-on learning and multiple opportunities to experience and practice tasks are the best way for young children with intellectual disabilities to learn. Individual motivation is also important. Here are some specific instructional strategies to use.

Be as concrete as possible. A child with an intellectual disability may not understand what is expected the first time you ask him to do something. In addition to verbal directions, use visual, tactile, and physical prompts to help him understand what you want him to do. For example, when you tell the children to line up (verbal cue), show a photograph of children standing in line (visual cue) and have cutouts of cardboard feet or rubber mats on the floor where you want them to stand (tactile cue). These adaptations will make the direction to "line up" more concrete for the child with an intellectual disability and may help everyone else, too.

Whenever possible, use manipulatives when teaching academic skills. Manipulatives give students a tangible way to learn early math skills such as counting, comparing, and patterning.

Give immediate and specific feedback. When a child is learning a task, offer immediate, specific feedback so she can link her actions with what you're telling her about what she did. When she receives feedback while still thinking about the task, both the task and the feedback are more meaningful for the child, and she can use what you say to understand whether she accomplished the task or needs to make corrections. Use feedback that is specific to the task ("You put both your feet on the right spot. Now I know you're ready to go!") and not generic ("Good job").

For example, if you are helping Kaito learn the morning arrival routine, one step might be for him to put his backpack in his cubby. Provide a few prompts at the same time:

» Verbal prompt: "Put your backpack away, Kaito."

» Visual prompt: Point to a photo of his backpack in his cubby.

» Tactile prompt: Pat his backpack while he still has it on.

As Kaito puts his backpack in his cubby, respond with, "You are putting your backpack in your cubby, Kaito. Thank you!" Repeat this until he can put away his backpack with no prompts.

Break down tasks into smaller steps. Teaching a task one step at a time, gradually adding each step, makes it easier for a child with an intellectual disability to understand and follow the sequence. A skill can be taught forward or backward. Say, for example, a child is learning to put on a pair of sweatpants by himself.

» **Teaching the skill forward:** Start with teaching the child the first step in the process: putting one leg at a time inside of each of the correct leg holes while he is sitting down. When he masters this, add the next step: pulling the pants up until his feet come out of the leg holes at the bottom and the waistband rests on his hips. Have the child do these first two steps together until he can do them himself. Continue teaching each step in turn—like standing up and then pulling the pants up to his waist—always adding on to the steps already learned, until you teach him all of the steps from the beginning to the end and the child can put his pants on by himself.

» **Teaching the skill backward:** Here you teach the child to do the very *last* step in a task first, like pulling his sweatpants up to his waist by himself. Do the beginning steps of putting on the sweatpants (putting one leg at a time in each leg hole, pulling the pants up until his feet emerge from the leg holes, etc.) for the child, and let him do the last step himself. When he's achieved this, do everything but the last *two* steps, and so on until you teach all of the steps from the end to the beginning, with the child mastering one step at a time.

Both techniques—teaching a skill forward or backward—are effective. Some children may prefer one way over the other, or it may be easier to teach some skills one way or the other. Whichever method you choose, remember to teach just one step at a time.

Teach play skills and early academic skills. Play is an essential skill for learning and also for socializing with others. While most children learn to play naturally, some children with intellectual disabilities tend to use materials in simpler ways and have difficulty engaging in more meaningful interactions. They may need your help to learn how to play with toys and with other children (Astramovich, Lyons, & Hamilton 2015; Barton 2015; Ferreira, Mäkinen, & Amorim 2016).

Teaching a child how to play involves spending one-to-one time with the child and taking the lead in play to show her what you want her to do. Invite the child to do what you do, offer lots of repetition, and slowly remove supports as the child learns to do the action on her own. For example, if a child does not yet play with objects in meaningful ways, teach her to imitate your actions with toys—putting a peg in the pegboard, rolling a car back and forth—and once the child imitates these actions, expand to more complex ones, like rolling the car along a road on the rug.

Parallel play—in which children play by themselves but near others using similar materials—is important because it helps children learn to share play spaces with each other. To teach a child with an intellectual disability to play alongside other children, start by having him parallel play with you first. For example, join him at the sand table and play next to him. Another time, move to play at the sand table first and then have another adult prompt the child to play alongside you. Finally, introduce another child to the play at the sand table.

Similarly, to teach a child with an intellectual disability more interactive play skills, start by trading or sharing toys with the child, prompting her if necessary. Use toys the child enjoys playing with. Introduce sharing and turn taking, and gradually bring in another adult or a peer. Cooperative play is more difficult for many children with intellectual disabilities because it often requires more complex thinking and imagining than the child has developed. Find ways for a child to play with his peers, such as asking them what role he could play in their firefighter scenario.

Using tablets and apps to teach and reinforce academic skills. Tablets and other touchscreen technology can be very easy to use and highly motivating for some children with intellectual disabilities. Customized to meet each student's needs, they can be used as part of assistive technology (AT) to teach academics in the early primary grades (Bouck et al. 2012).

Some commercially available early learning apps provide immediate feedback about correct or incorrect answers. This gives students a chance to practice early academic math and literacy skills independently in school or at home. There are also AT apps that help make certain academic tasks easier for a child. For example, a student whose poor small motor skills make it difficult to write can use specific AT tools to select answers or write without a pencil.

Encouraging Friendships

Learning to play with peers is the first step in helping children with intellectual disabilities develop early friendships. Set the stage for budding friendships by providing

» Cooperative toys that work best or are more fun when two or more children use them together, such as wagons, balls, puppets, and swings

» Opportunities for two children to work together during the day, like passing out scarves or rhythm instruments at group time or holding hands while walking to another part of the building. Use a buddy system: identify buddies for the day and have specific buddy activities, such as art projects. Change up the pairings so all children have the chance to get to know each other better.

» Strategies for joining other children in play. Teach a child with an intellectual disability to ask, "May I play with you?" to another child or group of children.

Preventing Challenging Behaviors

Because young children with intellectual disabilities lack some of the key skills needed to do what others are doing—communicate clearly, solve problems, understand social cues—they are more likely to exhibit challenging behavior than children without disabilities are (Heward 2012). The more severe the intellectual disability, the more likely this is. Self-injurious behaviors (such as hitting, scratching, and biting themselves) and obsessive-compulsive acts (such as picking at skin or rocking back and forth) are common in children with severe intellectual disabilities (Heward 2012).

In some cases, challenging behaviors result from a child's inability to make his wants and needs understood. All children communicate in one form or another, whether with words, crying, gestures, or objects, pictures, and symbols—or even a combination of some or all of these methods—but it may not be enough for an adult or a peer to understand them.

If another person does not understand what the child is trying to communicate, the child may, in frustration, resort to other means of expressing himself. It is important to recognize this and to address the child's underlying need, not simply the behavior. The behavior reflects his lack of communication skills, so focus on improving those skills and helping the child learn more effective ways of getting his needs met.

To reduce the challenging behavior and support a child's communication skills, you can

» Give the child words to help him understand his own—and others'—feelings: "Mateo, you stomped your foot. Are you angry that Lucia took the book you wanted to look at? Let's see what we can do."

» Have the child use picture communication strategies, such as simple picture symbols or photos, as a way for her to communicate with adults and peers.

» Use activity schedules or visual supports to help the child transition from one task to another or as a visual cue to remind the child of the behavioral expectations in different settings.

» Provide computer-based instruction, such as a tablet and apps, to teach communication and social skills.

For more on addressing challenging behaviors, see Chapter 5.

Summary

Children with intellectual disabilities span a wide range of abilities and needs. Those with mild disabilities may need assistance in school, but many go on to have jobs and families and lead independent lives. Children with more severe intellectual disabilities, in particular those who also have other disabilities, continue to need a great deal of support throughout adulthood. While many people still view IQ scores as a firm predictor of a child's overall ability to learn and achieve, success or failure in school or life cannot be predicted by a test score or a medical diagnosis. Evaluate what the child can do and learn, and maximize the learning potential of every child by having high expectations based on each child's desires, abilities, and needs.

11 Attention-Deficit/ Hyperactivity Disorder

Mr. and Mrs. Wynne are concerned about their son, Marcus. He is a handful sometimes, especially in church, where he just cannot seem to keep still, or in the grocery store, where he loves to run up and down the aisles. They know that it's important for him to be active, but Marcus is in the first grade now and his parents worry that his behavior might cause problems in school. They decide to meet with his teacher, Mrs. Collins.

They share their concerns with Mrs. Collins, and she explains that she has noticed that Marcus has difficulty regulating his attention during the day, like stopping one activity to shift his focus to another or finishing his classwork in the same time as the other students. Mrs. Collins has been keeping data on this, which shows that Marcus's behavior is not improving over time. She encourages his parents to see their son's pediatrician.

Mr. and Mrs. Wynne talk to Dr. Lee about Mrs. Collins's observations and what Marcus is like at home. After talking extensively with Mr. and Mrs. Wynne, reviewing the data shared by Mrs. Collins, and spending time playing with Marcus, Dr. Lee tells Mr. and Mrs. Wynne that she is comfortable giving Marcus a diagnosis of attention-deficit/hyperactivity disorder (ADHD).

Mr. and Mrs. Wynne are surprised at first, then apprehensive. They have heard about children with this diagnosis and don't want to put Marcus on any medications. Dr. Lee agrees that medication is not the right treatment at this time, and she encourages them to work with Marcus's school to teach him how to regulate his own behavior and provide him with some tools that will help him in school and at home.

When Mr. and Mrs. Wynne tell Mrs. Collins about the diagnosis, she reaches out to one of her colleagues, Mr. Poivre, for suggestions on modifying the classroom activities and routines to help Marcus. On his advice, Mrs. Collins changes the class schedule to make it very predictable every day. She also adds a large visual timer on the SMART board so that everyone can see the red circle getting smaller and smaller to signify that time is almost up for an activity. Another idea she

implements is to have the class return to a home base after each activity to review and to check what's next on the schedule, then celebrate their finished task with a 2-minute dance party for everyone to get their bodies moving.

Mr. Poivre also gives Mrs. Collins some ideas to help Marcus specifically, like breaking down each assignment into smaller chunks and giving him a checklist so he can mark off when he completes each part. Marcus loves this, as it gives him a sense of accomplishment and helps him finish tasks almost as quickly as the other students.

Seeing how these changes help Marcus in school, his parents find some apps for visual timers on their phones and start to use checklists in the morning to help him get ready for school and in the afternoon for his homework and chores. They even discover how fun it is to have a few dance parties of their own at home, too!

As Marcus's parents understand, all young children learn actively through moving and exploring the environment as well as manipulating and experimenting with objects to construct their own understanding about the world around them. All children get restless, have difficulty paying attention, daydream, or act impulsively at times, but as Mrs. Collins noted about Marcus, children with ADHD have difficulties with some of these behaviors more frequently than other children do (ED 2008). By age 4, most children begin to develop the ability to self-regulate—that is, to focus their attention on a person or an activity, control their emotions, and manage their behavior and impulses to be part of a group setting—but children with attention disorders have trouble with this skill.

ADHD symptoms can persist for a long time, sometimes into adulthood. Although working with medical professionals and families to figure out when there is a true attention problem can be challenging, it's very important to identify a child who needs intervention. Early identification and support can help a child learn to manage his behavior and maximize his chances for success.

What Is ADHD?

ADHD is a medical diagnosis that impacts about 5 percent of the population (APA 2013); the CDC estimates that 11 percent of children ages 4 through 17 are affected (Visser et al. 2015). According to the *Diagnostic and Statistical Manual of Mental Disorders*, Fifth Edition (DSM-5; APA 2013) there are three types of ADHD:

» **Inattentive ADHD** is usually identified in children who are easily distracted or very inattentive. This type is what people commonly refer to as ADD (attention deficit disorder) since the child usually shows no signs of hyperactivity or impulsivity. A child with inattentive ADHD doesn't seem to listen to directions or misses important details, or she is unorganized and unable to find her possessions or the materials she needs.

» **Hyperactive-impulsive ADHD** is usually identified in children who are restless and reckless but not inattentive. A child with hyperactive-impulsive ADHD may fidget and have difficulty sitting still; he may constantly interrupt conversations and speak out of turn.

» **Combined ADHD** describes children who demonstrate inattention, hyperactivity, *and* impulsivity. You may notice a child who is unable to remain seated for a long period of time, is forgetful, and has difficulty following through on a task or assignment.

Many children are diagnosed with ADHD when they are in the early primary grades, although signs often appear much earlier. As many as 40 percent of children who eventually receive a diagnosis of ADHD show signs by age 4, making ADHD the most common mental health disorder that is identified at that age (Visser et al. 2015).

ADHD is considered a health impairment under IDEA if it impacts a child's educational performance. Some children who don't qualify under IDEA but need extra help in the classroom might receive services under Section 504 of the Rehabilitation Act of 1973 (Public Law 93-112). This law defines *disability* more broadly than IDEA and prohibits any program that receives federal funding assistance from discriminating against people with disabilities. ADHD is *not* a learning disability (Cortiella & Horowitz 2014). Chapter 12 discusses learning disabilities.

Possible Reasons for ADHD

ADHD is not a problem caused by lenient or ineffective parents or schools or by too much screen time. Children with ADHD do not just need consistency or a firm hand and consequences to "get over" their ADHD and improve their behavior.

ADHD is a biological condition (APA 2013). While there is no single cause, there is a strong genetic component to ADHD, which means that it often runs in families. Some environmental factors, such as exposure to maternal smoking and drinking in utero or to pesticides or lead during infancy, may play a role in the development of ADHD in some children (APA 2013). Premature birth may also put a child at risk. Research is ongoing to help determine how biological and environmental factors might work together to cause the condition.

Impact of ADHD on Development and Learning

Attention disorders impact the way children interact with their environment and peers and can inhibit the way they learn. Sometimes the child is labeled a troublemaker or a problem kid. A child who struggles with inattentiveness and distractibility may have trouble hearing and following directions or focusing on an activity or lesson and completing it. He may constantly misplace things—his shoes, his homework—causing frustration for himself and others. His impulsiveness can lead to interrupting others, having difficulty taking turns, lashing out at others, or getting into unsafe situations. All of this can aggravate adults and peers, and a child with ADHD often has trouble gaining the acceptance of others, resulting in low self-esteem (Mayo Clinic 2016a). Because children with ADHD often act younger than their age, they may find it difficult to form friendships with their same-age peers; many gravitate to children who are younger than they are.

Identifying ADHD

When a child has a difficult time transitioning from more active times of the day to less active times, is always on the go and can't settle down, or exhibits other behaviors outside the norm, some adults assume that it must be ADHD. There are other conditions with similar symptoms, however, and a medical doctor—who must do a full evaluation to determine whether a child has ADHD—usually explores and rules out other possible conditions before diagnosing ADHD. These include undetected seizures, hypothyroidism, trauma, learning disabilities, problems with motor or communication skills, and psychological or behavioral disorders like anxiety and bipolar disorder (Bhatia 2016; NIMH 2008).

A diagnosis of ADHD should follow a thorough medical exam and complete review of medical history, a checklist rating of the symptoms, and input from parents and teachers about the child's behaviors at home and school. The child's symptoms must cause impairment across more than one setting; if the child has difficulty only at school or only at home, there is likely something else occurring (Subcommittee on ADHD 2011).

The American Academy of Pediatrics (AAP; Subcommittee on ADHD 2011) discourages pediatricians from diagnosing ADHD in children younger than 4 years old. This is largely because it is difficult to distinguish between a very active toddler or preschooler and one who has ADHD (MacDonald 2015). However, signs of ADHD can appear early, and parents, teachers, and doctors often go back to review those early signs and symptoms when considering an initial diagnosis of ADHD. Although the AAP offers guidelines for diagnosing children as young as age 4, many doctors will not do a full evaluation for ADHD until the child is school age (Subcommittee on ADHD 2011).

ADHD symptoms in preschoolers. The following signs, if present for more than six months, may indicate that a 3- or 4-year-old may have ADHD (Kennedy Krieger Institute 2012):

- » **Delays in physical development:** Unable to hop on one foot
- » **Risk taking:** Shows little or no fear in dangerous situations, sometimes resulting in serious injury. Befriends strangers easily, with no fear or caution.
- » **Short attention span:** Cannot play for longer than a few minutes, leaves the activity quickly, or refuses to participate in lengthier activities. Unable to sit without squirming, frequently needs to move.
- » **Difficulty making similar-age friends:** Louder and noisier than other children they are playing with. May show aggressive behavior when playing with peers.

ADHD symptoms in school-age children. Teachers are often instrumental in identifying a child's symptoms, such as the following (Bolyn 2015):

- » **Inattention:** Needs daily reminders to complete his classwork. Has a hard time concentrating on an activity that he does not enjoy.
- » **Being impulsive:** Interrupts others when they are talking and has a hard time following rules. Makes decisions and acts without thinking things through first.
- » **Being hyperactive:** Has a hard time staying still all day; constantly in motion, like tapping her feet or wiggling in her chair.

Treatments and Therapies for ADHD

Both medical and nonmedical treatments are used to help children with ADHD. Professionals in many different fields may be involved in a child's treatment, including physicians, psychologists, social workers, therapists, and educators.

Medication

For many years, a common treatment for ADHD symptoms has been the use of prescription stimulant medications. These increase levels of chemicals in the brain, particularly dopamine, which are often lower in children with ADHD (Cleveland Clinic 2013). Between 70 and 80 percent of school-age children diagnosed with ADHD take a stimulant medication, such as Ritalin or Adderall (Visser et al. 2015). Nonstimulant medications are also available.

Many families and teachers have found that these medications give short-term help to school-age children, enabling them to sit still and concentrate better in school. However, there is no long-term evidence that academic achievement and behavior are changed by taking medication for ADHD, and many children experience significant side effects like loss of appetite and insomnia (Visser et al. 2015). Strategies that focus on helping a child change her behavior, on the other hand, can give her skills that will benefit her long term.

Nonmedical Treatments for ADHD

Nonmedical strategies focus on ways to change the environment, routines, and expectations to accommodate children's needs, rather than trying to make children fit into the current structure of the classroom or home.

> » **Behavioral supports.** A system of positive behavior supports, which includes a solid structure of predictable schedules, routines, and expectations, is often the most effective short- and long-term strategy for young children. You might give a child a report card each day that shows how well he met his goals, like finishing his homework or speaking only when it's his turn. When he meets his goals, he gets a reward.

> » **Social skills supports.** Intentionally teach the specific social and emotional skills children may not have yet. You can manipulate how routines or activities are done so that, for example, two students must collaborate as a way to practice problem solving (Lentini, Vaughn, & Fox 2005). When children learn to understand their own and others' emotions, handle conflicts, problem solve, and develop relationships with peers, their challenging behavior decreases and their social skills improve (Fox & Lentini 2006).

> » **Supports at home.** Parents can help their children regulate their behavior by having clear rules; using praise and rewards when children follow the rules and providing clearly understood and reinforced consequences when they don't; providing predictable routines; helping children manage their time and possessions; and giving simple instructions. When teachers and families share information about how a child is doing and use similar strategies at home and school, the child is more likely to be successful.

Children with ADHD often hear what they're doing wrong. Remember to build on children's abilities and give them positive encouragement when they're doing well!

You probably know at least one child who can't seem to get enough of jumping or swinging or bouncing, who is always moving some part of her body, who *has* to touch everyone and everything, who often gets hurt but seems unaffected by pain. Or a child who can't stand wearing his blue shirt with the itchy tag, who hears every background noise that no one else pays attention to—the air conditioner humming, fluorescent lights buzzing—and is driven crazy by it.

Many of these children have **sensory processing issues.** They react strongly to information coming in from their senses—touch, sight, hearing, smelling, and tasting, plus the vestibular (sense of balance/dizziness) and proprioceptive (knowing your body position and where your body is in space) senses—in ways most children don't. They may be oversensitive, seeking to avoid stimulation because it's overwhelming, or under-sensitive, craving an experience that gives them that stimulation. They may be both.

What Are Sensory Processing Issues?

The brain receives all kinds of messages from each of the senses, and the brain interprets these messages to help us make meaning from them. Children who have sensory processing issues often aren't able to filter out less important information, or they have trouble organizing information coming in from multiple senses at once (Kranowitz 2016). Some children process all of the information equally until they become overloaded with sensory messages and are unable to make sense of any of them.

Children may have problems processing information from just a few senses. For example, a child who does not like to eat certain foods because of the texture may have no problems with balance or noisy environments. Reactions are sometimes inconsistent, extreme one day and mild the next (Kranowitz 2016; Leigh 2016).

Many children with delays or disabilities, including those with ASD and ADHD, experience sensory processing issues (Palmer 2014; Reynolds, Lane, & Gennings 2009), and these issues are recognized as a symptom of these disorders. They can also occur in children with no diagnosed disability, although they are not considered a disability under IDEA or a separate disorder in DSM-5. However, these issues can greatly affect children's learning and behavior, making it difficult for them to feel secure, concentrate, and socialize.

What Does a Sensory Processing Issue Look Like?

Sensory issues are different for each child. Children who are very sensitive to stimulation may show defensive behaviors like these:

- Refusing certain food textures
- Showing distress when their diaper or clothing is changed
- Not wanting other people to touch them
- Being extremely bothered by bright lights and loud sounds, like sirens or a vacuum cleaner, or even subtler sounds like a refrigerator hum
- Avoiding or becoming uncomfortable in large, noisy groups
- Balking at transitions to a different activity or place
- Avoiding elevators, amusement park rides, or even car rides because they get motion sickness easily

Children who are under-sensitive to stimuli may compensate for their need for more stimulation by seeking it out. With these children, you might see behaviors such as the following:

- Wanting to be swaddled, have heavy blankets, or tight pajamas for sleeping
- Needing to be rocked, bounced, or have their back rubbed to get to sleep
- Frequently touching things or people, not understanding boundaries
- Wanting and giving tight hugs
- Fidgeting with something in their hands; trouble sitting still
- Seeking out thrill rides, wanting to go fast, spin, or be upside down; not getting dizzy (Child Mind Institute 2017b; SPD Support 2017)

Because sensory processing issues are not considered a separate disorder, identifying the problem and finding help can be difficult for families. Occupational therapists are generally the ones to evaluate a child and may provide a diagnosis of sensory processing disorder based on assessment tools, observations of the child's functional activities, and conversations with the child's family and teachers.

Strategies for Therapy and the Classroom

An occupational therapist may design a therapeutic approach—known as **sensory integration therapy**—to help a child learn to integrate and regulate sensory information. The therapist works with a child on activities like spinning, bouncing, and deep pressure that is calming. Although no studies prove that sensory integration works for children, many families do see improvement with therapy (Child Mind Institute 2017c).

Here are a few things teachers and families can do to help children be more comfortable and successful in the classroom and at home:

- Keep things active by letting children move whenever possible.
- Provide security items (blanket, stuffed toy) to help a child learn how to self-regulate in situations that are overstimulating or otherwise causing anxiety (Passman 1977). Let older children keep something in their hands to fidget with.
- Provide sensory spaces—places in the room where a child can remove herself from overwhelming sensory stimulation. Make a quiet, cozy area with carpeting that makes the child feel more enclosed and reduces stimulation.
- Make sure the child's chair fits her, and she can put her feet flat on the floor and rest her elbows on the desk. Some children may need seating options that let them move more, like bouncy balls.
- Check that overhead lighting is not flickering or buzzing and that noises from the heater and air conditioner are not distracting a child.
- Have a strategy for large groups, like the lunchroom and assemblies. They may be overwhelming to some children. It may be okay for the child to miss a one-time event or sit near the door or on a quieter side of the room with just a few friends.
- Use visual schedules to help children prepare for transitions (Child Mind Institute 2017a).

It is important to understand each child's sensory needs to help her develop the necessary self-regulation and self-soothing skills for home and school. Close collaboration between the child's family, therapist, and teacher will help provide the support the child needs.

Strategies for the Classroom

Here are some strategies that can help a child with ADHD make positive behavior changes in the classroom:

» **Identify exactly what a child has difficulty with.** Can she start an activity just fine, but has trouble following through with it? Does she get distracted by too many materials in her work or play space? Provide supports in those areas where she most struggles.

» **Follow a routine.** A structured, predictable routine helps children with ADHD know what to expect. This supports their self-regulation skills.

  • Post a visual schedule for the routines and activities of the day.

  • Have a simple, consistent routine for each part of your day. When a child comes into the classroom each morning, he knows what to do. When a child is done with his classwork, he knows where to put his work.

  • Add a home-base routine to the schedule. For example, when a lesson or an activity is completed, have everyone meet back at the rug or other central location before moving to the next activity.

» **Get organized.** Children with ADHD often have problems deciding what's important and how to prioritize tasks. These skills are part of what is called *executive function*.

  • Have a place for everything and make sure everything is in its place. A clear system of organization around the classroom makes everything run smoother and helps children be more independent.

  • Use colors to show what is important. For example, folders that are red must go home each day.

  • Give older children a master binder with everything color coded, and teach them how to write down homework assignments.

» **Give directions one at a time.** If there's more than one step to a task, try making each one a separate task so the child has a sense of accomplishment as she finishes each task.

» **Allow plenty of time.** Children with ADHD often need more time to complete routines and activities than other children do. Make sure children are not rushed through their routines. Give them plenty of time and advance notice before transitions to make changing activities as smooth as possible.

» **Identify the steps in a process.** Children with inattention or impulsivity often skip steps in a process. Teach the child the steps she needs to complete—for example, what to do before leaving at the end of the day. A visual checklist is helpful for teaching these skills.

Large motor play and movement are not just good for the heart and muscles; they're also good for the brain. Even light physical activity, such as dancing to music in the classroom or going for a walk outside, can trigger the brain to release the neurotransmitter dopamine—the same intent as the prescription stimulant medications used to treat ADHD (Hamblin 2014; Hillman et al. 2014). Purposely adding physical activities to a child's day can make her more aware of her own body and how to regulate her movements, which can have a calming effect (Hamblin 2014; Kranowitz 2016).

Here are some additional ideas:

- Set up obstacle courses where children can go over, under, around, and through objects, focusing on balance and coordination skills. Use bubble wrap in your obstacle course so children can jump on it and pop it!
- Play games that require following directions and regulating movement, like Twister or Simon Says.
- Encourage children to throw and catch a ball with you or each other. This engages both the body and the brain, developing a child's focus and organizational skills.

» **Provide a place to be alone.** Sometimes children need to de-stress, and teaching them how to do this for themselves is invaluable.

- Give children a safe, private place to calm down when needed.
- Teach the child to use this space when he feels overwhelmed. Do not treat the space as punishment.

» **Set a good example.** Keep things positive for the child, and have a set of "dos" that you teach the child instead of always telling her what *not* to do.

- Try not to let the child see you stressed and anxious. Show her what you expect her to do in as relaxed a manner as possible.
- Model the need to take a step back and de-escalate your own feelings.

Summary

Attention disorders are real medical issues, but medication is not always the best solution for young children. Nonprescription interventions—including behavioral, social, and home supports—are usually most appropriate. Changing some routines and activities of your day so children can move and engage their muscles *and* brains also helps them learn to regulate their own behavior and actions.

Even with supports in place, working with children who display attention issues can be challenging. Remember that children are not acting a certain way on purpose. Helping them learn how to regulate their own behavior will make all the difference to you and them.

12 Learning Disabilities

Ziad is a bright, athletic third grade boy who loves school, but his teacher, Mr. Washington, is unsure what to do about his learning disability. It seems that no matter what techniques he tries, Ziad still struggles with understanding what he reads.

Mr. Washington asks Mrs. Ellicott, the special education teacher who works with Ziad, for help. Mrs. Ellicott observes Ziad in class for a few days and then talks to Mr. Washington to outline some strategies that might work.

The first strategy the teacher tries is called pause-think-retell. Mr. Washington decides to use this with everyone in Ziad's reading group. After a few scenes of the story, the group stops to think for a few minutes, and then they retell, in their own words or by drawing pictures, what happened so far in the story, details about the characters, or other information. Mr. Washington very much likes this strategy since he can monitor each child in the group and see how much detail each recalls. The first few times, no one in the group recalls much, so they reread the story and try the pause-think-retell strategy again.

After a few more weeks of using this strategy, Ziad's comprehension starts to improve and he becomes more confident in his understanding of what he reads. Like Mr. Washington, Ziad likes the pause-think-retell strategy, and best of all, he know it's working for him. He even starts to use it when reading his science textbook for homework. Knowing that he uses this strategy on his own makes Mr. Washington very proud of Ziad, and he tells him so.

Academic challenges and learning difficulties are common problems. Some academic challenges go hand in hand with intellectual, physical, or other identified disabilities. When a child who has no other identified disabilities has difficulty with reading, writing, spelling, and/or organizing or recalling information, however, he may have a learning disability. One in every seven Americans (15 percent) has a learning disability, and 8 to 10 percent of school-age children under the age of 18 have been diagnosed with a learning disability and receive special education services in school (NICHD 2017a).

What Are Learning Disabilities?

Learning disabilities are not a single disorder but more a general description of difficulties with processing certain kinds of information. There are several different types of learning disabilities, and many children have more than one.

» **Dyslexia** is a language-based disability in which a person has trouble understanding how speech sounds relate to letters and words.

» **Dyscalculia** is a mathematical disability in which a person has a difficult time understanding and solving arithmetic problems as well as understanding math concepts and learning math facts.

» **Dysgraphia** is a motor planning/writing disability in which a person finds it hard to recognize how to form different letters and to write words on paper.

» **Nonverbal learning disability** is a disorder in which a person finds it hard to interpret nonverbal communication; she may also have difficulty understanding how ideas relate to each other and generalizing a concept to different situations.

Researchers believe that people with learning disabilities have a neurological disorder in which the brain is wired a bit differently, causing trouble with processing, organizing, and interpreting the information they receive from their senses as well as recalling, organizing, and relaying information to others (Kane 2012). For example, when a child sees a word on a page, that information is relayed to his brain to see if the word has already been learned. If so, the brain instantly finds the word, and the child is able to read the word effortlessly. However, a child with a learning disability will see the word on the page, but his brain struggles to find the word in his memory (even if he has learned the word before), and he has difficulty reading the word. These same processing issues can happen when a child tries to understand math facts, process and express language, or engage in other areas of learning (Flink 2014).

As children start the primary grades, more of the information they learn comes through their eyes (reading a book, watching what the teacher is writing on the board) or through their ears (listening to the teacher give directions). The more information the brain is asked to process at the same time, the more noticeable it is when that process is not working correctly. These types of demands are why learning disabilities are often not diagnosed until a child is in the primary grades. There is usually a discrepancy between the child's potential to learn and what she actually learns.

Possible Reasons for Learning Disabilities

The precise cause of learning disabilities is unknown, but heredity seems to be a factor. Other possible risk factors are exposure to drugs or alcohol during pregnancy, illness or injury before or during birth, or exposure to lead (NICHD 2017b).

Impact of Learning Disabilities on Development and Learning

Children with learning disabilities struggle with skills that affect them at school, at home, and in social situations. Reading, writing, and math may be difficult, as well as understanding what other people are saying. A child may have trouble with abstract reasoning and seeing the big picture. Weaknesses in visual and spatial perception may affect not only schoolwork but also coordination and participation in sports. Inside and outside of school, children may struggle with being on time, keeping organized, and having social interactions. Helping children develop the needed skills and strategies when they are young is essential.

When a child experiences frustration because learning is difficult and classmates seem to have an easier time, she may become depressed or angry. Common challenging behaviors include resisting doing homework or constantly asking for step-by-step help with homework that involves an area of difficulty, like math; showing excessive emotional reactions at school or home about homework or other challenging activities; and frequently misplacing or losing school books or other items to avoid homework (Mayo Clinic 2016c).

It's important that children—and educators—understand that people who have learning disabilities are not dumb or lazy. Learning disabilities are not a reflection of a person's intelligence or level of effort. Individuals with learning disabilities generally have average or above-average intelligence and often have to work much harder at tasks other people take for granted, like reading. They also have many strengths, often in areas not emphasized in academic settings. With the right support and encouragement to use their strengths as a foundation for learning, they can be successful both in and out of school (YCDC 2017).

Facts about learning disabilities

- It's estimated that 15 percent of the people in the United States have some sort of learning disability, but only 5 percent have been identified.
- Reading disabilities are the most common form of learning disabilities.
- Learning disabilities often occur in multiple members of the same family. (Cortiella & Horowitz 2014)

Identifying Learning Disabilities

Diagnosing a learning disability is not an exact science; it's a bit like putting together a complex puzzle. Some methods of diagnosing a learning disability rely heavily on the professional judgment of the person evaluating the child, and that naturally varies from professional to professional. In addition, states may have different criteria and standards for identifying and diagnosing learning disabilities in schools, and it is possible that a student would be identified as having a learning disability in one state but not another.

Comprehensive Assessments

When evaluating a child for learning disabilities, professionals use both cognitive assessments and academic achievement measures. **Cognitive assessments** are commonly referred to as intelligence quotient (IQ) tests and measure thinking, problem-solving skills, and the child's overall ability and potential to learn compared to other children the same age. **Academic achievement tests** measure the basic academic skills a child has compared with other children the same age.

Dispelling the dyslexia myth
The misconception persists that dyslexia is characterized by letters and words appearing to reverse or switch places, and that this is responsible for reading difficulties. However, research shows that dyslexia is more about sounds than written letters. People with dyslexia have trouble discriminating basic sounds of speech, called *phonemes,* which are part of all spoken and written words (Mayo Clinic 2014b). This makes it difficult for an individual to connect letters and sounds to read a word.

A comprehensive assessment for learning disabilities should *always* include other sources of information, including informal classroom-based assessments, observations of the student in class, student self-reports if they are old enough, and parent accounts of the child's functioning at home. If the multiple sources of information indicate that a student's learning needs are not due to a vision or hearing loss, an intellectual disability, social-emotional difficulties, limited English proficiency, or a lack of opportunities to attend school or learn *and* the student is not achieving adequately for his age, then the IEP team can determine that there is a learning disability (NJCLD 2010).

Early Signs of Learning Disabilities

Teachers and families should be aware of some of the early signs of learning disabilities. The Learning Disabilities Association of America (LDA; 2017) and the National Association of Special Education Teachers (NASET; 2017) are among many organizations that have published lists of early symptoms of learning disabilities. Although most learning disabilities are not diagnosed until the child is in the early primary grades, it is always better to express concerns early than to wait.

Here are a few signs that a child may be at risk for a learning disability.

Preschool

- » Struggles to pronounce words
- » Repeatedly misidentifies common known sight words (classmates' names, classroom labels)
- » Doesn't identify or recognize rhyming patterns in easy words like *cat, bat,* and *rat*
- » Has difficulty with routines and following directions
- » Has difficulty with small motor control like holding a pencil or zipping a jacket
- » Has trouble sorting items by size, shape, or color, or repeating simple patterns

Kindergarten and First Grade

- » Has difficulty associating written letters with sounds
- » Has trouble segmenting words into syllables or clapping out syllables
- » Exhibits challenging behavior or other kinds of avoidance (pretending to feel sick) when it is time to read
- » Has difficulty with comprehension
- » Consistently shows spelling or reading errors like letter reversals (*b/d*), inversions (*m/w*), transpositions (*felt/left*), and substitutions (*house/home*)
- » Struggles with math concepts, such as *greater than* and *less than*
- » Has a hard time telling his left from his right and has a poor sense of direction

Second Grade and Up

- » Reads aloud very slowly and awkwardly; often reads word by word with no inflection
- » Makes wild guesses on unknown words to avoid having to sound them out
- » Uses vague language such as "stuff" or "thing" a lot
- » Needs extra time to respond to oral questions
- » Can't recall previously learned basic math facts, such as 2 + 2 = 4
- » Has difficulty writing numerals in math problems, specifically putting them in the correct column

When considering whether a child's difficulties may signal a learning disability, it's

important to take into account the opportunities he's had to learn the skills in question. If a child has had little exposure to rhyming words—reading and sound play do not occur often at home, and he has experienced few group learning settings—it is unfair to assume that the child must be having difficult learning. However, if a child has had ample opportunities and still has difficulty, it is more likely that the problem is not due to lack of exposure.

Strategies for the Classroom

When a student is struggling, you do not need to wait for formal testing to confirm that current instruction is not working for this student. Even if a child has not been identified with a learning disability, consider what you can do now to support her. Keep in mind that no single method will help all students. Effective teaching requires intense, individualized methods that are beyond the scope of this chapter to address. Be intentional, systematic, and patient as you try strategies with a particular child.

Working with Strengths

Children with learning disabilities have many strengths that you can draw on in the classroom to help them experience success in learning and increase their self-esteem.

Preschool, Kindergarten, and First Grade

» Work with the child's natural curiosity about new materials and concepts, and encourage her to figure things out for herself.

» Provide many opportunities for the child to use his imagination to design and create.

» Read aloud stories that are above children's own reading levels. Most students with learning disabilities have a high level of understanding and a sophisticated listening vocabulary.

Second Grade and Up

» Learn what children are interested in and have them read about whatever it is. Reading confidence is buoyed by interest, motivation, and vocabulary words that are frequently practiced.

» Emphasize big-picture skills like reasoning, imagination, and abstraction rather than rote memorization of ideas and facts.

» Continue to read to children from books that are more difficult than they can read independently.

» Provide opportunities for children to find success in areas that do not depend on skills they have trouble with, such as visual arts, dramatic arts, or sports. Remind them that they are more than their ability to do classwork.

Tiered Systems of Support

In an effort to provide children with systematic, targeted interventions before they fall so far behind academically that they qualify for special education, many states and schools have developed tiered systems of support for K–12 programs. These systems are most commonly referred to as **response to intervention** (RTI) or multi-tiered systems of support (MTSS) programs (Samuels 2016). The programs are usually founded on

» High-quality, evidence-based curriculum and instruction at every level

» Ongoing assessment of students, including universal screening several times a year and progress monitoring

» Multiple levels, or tiers, of support and instruction with increasingly targeted interventions before a child is referred for a special education evaluation (RTI Action Network 2017)

While RTI programs are very popular in schools and many are implemented based on good intentions, there are some concerns about the model's effectiveness. RTI has not been empirically validated; it is more of a theory that schools implement based on their own design than a model that identifies specific intervention (Sparks 2015). A recent study by the US Department of Education found that even when implemented as intended, many RTI programs do not reach the intended goals, and many students fall further behind their grade level rather than catch up (Balu et al. 2015).

It is important to understand that participating in tiered systems of support is not the same as, nor is it a substitute for, special education. Despite the shortcomings of some RTI implementations, the idea is built on designing teaching practices that give each child the support she needs to be successful at learning.

Working with Parents to Add Opportunities to Practice Skills at Home

Children from preschool through the early primary grades do well when they have repeated opportunities to practice skills they are learning every day. Encourage families to provide developmentally appropriate interactions and experiences that support the development of concepts and skills, such as

» Talking with their children about what they're doing, what they like, and what they're experiencing. Help parents understand how to ask higher-level questions that get children thinking, making connections, and using more complex language.

» Providing novel materials for children to explore, from everyday items like cartons and buttons, to objects they can take apart, explore, and use the parts to make new things. Exploring how things work stimulates conversations, collaboration, and problem-solving skills.

» Talking about simple chores the child can complete at home that involve early math skills, like setting the table for dinner and giving each person the correct place setting or matching and sorting the laundry.

» Reading aloud to their children, even when they're in the early primary grades. Encourage families to do shared reading, where an adult reads aloud and children are actively involved in answering questions or predicting what will happen next.

» Allowing their children to tinker with open-ended materials and build in makerspaces. Spaces can be set up at home, and some communities and libraries host them. These spaces encourage creativity, problem solving, and innovation, which are often strengths of children with learning disabilities.

Summary

Because academic challenges and difficulty with learning are common, there is a lot of information and support available for families, teachers, and students. Diagnosing learning disabilities can be a long process, but parents and teachers who believe a child might be displaying early symptoms should seek more information and provide supports that are developmentally appropriate and tailored to the child.

Teachers and parents can help children with learning disabilities achieve by encouraging them to understand their strengths as well as their barriers to learning, and teaching them to speak up for what they need (LDA 2017). Although learning disabilities do not go away, every person with a learning disability can employ strategies that will help her succeed in school, develop friendships, and have a successful career in the future.

Conclusion

It's the end of Alyssa's first year of teaching in Head Start, and she is exhausted but exhilarated. Chloe, who has spina bifida, has clearly thrived on the interaction with other children her own age and with the high-quality learning opportunities Alyssa provided. So have most of the other children in the classroom.

There have been plenty of challenging times. Unsure of how to support Jamari and Leo, Alyssa sought help from Mrs. Regan, who teaches across the hall and was an unofficial mentor for Alyssa throughout the year. Jamari's difficulty in communicating with the other children led to frustration and times when he acted out. Mrs. Regan helped Alyssa discover what triggered these behaviors, and together they problem-solved some ideas to address them. Alyssa gave Jamari extra time to process what she was saying and developed activities in which he and a classmate took turns talking. These non-stressful, enjoyable situations gave Jamari a role model for speech and helped him feel successful.

Leo's problems were a bit more challenging to address. At Mrs. Regan's suggestion, Alyssa focused on providing concrete activities and repetition so Leo could practice the skills he was learning. Although Leo continues to grasp concepts more slowly than the other children, Alyssa sees his progress. Since Leo will return to Head Start next year, Alyssa can continue monitoring how he's doing and providing supports. She realizes that Leo may need a referral for an evaluation next year.

Perhaps the most important thing Mrs. Regan has taught Alyssa, however, is to trust her instincts. She learned many of the things she needed in college, but it took time to trust that she was prepared to meet the needs of all the children in her class. Alyssa learned a lot throughout the year, and she knows she will continue to learn. As challenging as teaching is, she loves it more than she ever imagined and is confident that whatever comes her way next year, she can handle it.

Every child is unique. Every child is capable of learning something. Every child belongs.

Inclusion is not about the setting a child is educated in; it is a belief that all children are entitled to learn together and fully participate in their communities. You may be the first professional to suspect that a child may have a developmental delay or a disability and the first to implement interventions that will meet her developmental and educational needs. Whatever your situation, learn to trust your instincts and professional judgment, and know when to seek help from others who have valuable experience and knowledge to share with you. These are the most important things you can do for each child in your classroom.

Glossary

ABC: method of observing and analyzing a child's challenging behavior by considering the **a**ntecedent to the behavior, the **b**ehavior, and the **c**onsequence of the behavior

academic achievement tests: measures of a child's basic academic skills compared with other children the same age

access: policies put in place to make sure every student has an equal opportunity to take full advantage of an education; includes physical access, social and emotional access, and access to high-quality curriculum used by all learners

aided communication: the use of objects, pictures, photos, or specific devices to communicate

assistive technology (AT): specialized technology used as an individualized intervention to aid children's communication and learning

augmentative and alternative communication (AAC): devices that help children communicate, such as a picture board

behavior intervention plan (BIP): an individualized plan for addressing a child's challenging behavior by teaching missing skills and reinforcing appropriate replacement behaviors

braille: a system of raised dots that are read with the fingers

Child Find: a system required by IDEA to locate children who may have a disability and who would benefit from the state's early intervention or special education services

cognitive assessments: measures of a child's thinking, problem-solving skills, and overall ability and potential to learn compared to other children the same age; commonly referred to as intelligence quotient (IQ) tests

co-teaching: teaching arrangement in which a special education teacher and a general education teacher share teaching duties and responsibilities all day or for part of the day

developmental delay: a significant lag in achievement of developmental milestones

developmental disability: a severe, chronic mental or physical impairment (or both) that originates at birth or during childhood; is expected to continue indefinitely; and substantially restricts the individual's functioning in major life activities

developmentally appropriate practice (DAP): an approach to teaching based on research on how young children develop and learn and on what is known about effective early education. The approach takes into account children's age and developmental status, their unique strengths and needs, and the social and cultural contexts in which they live.

disability: a physical or mental condition that impacts the way the body works or develops, and significantly limits a person's abilities in one or more major life activities, including walking, standing, seeing, hearing, speaking, and/or learning

embedded learning: intentionally creating opportunities to work on specific therapeutic goals during classroom routines and activities

evidence-based practice (EBP): an intervention method proven to be consistently effective by scientifically based research

expressive language: the ways in which people use words or other means to communicate, like talking, gesturing, or signing

functional behavioral assessment (FBA): a process of gathering and analyzing data on a child's challenging behavior to identify why the behavior is occurring and what interventions decrease it

global developmental delay: a delay in at least two areas of development

identity-first language: a way of referring to an individual with a disability preferred by some people who have a disability; uses the disability word first to indicate that the disability is an important part of the individual (Deaf person, autistic person)

Individualized Education Program (IEP): written plan outlining a child's learning goals and services to be provided to meet the child's educational needs

Individualized Family Service Plan (IFSP): written plan for providing early intervention services for a young child and her family

inclusion: the practice of educating children with disabilities alongside their same-age peers who do not have disabilities

interdisciplinary team: a team of professionals who specialize in working with and evaluating a child to see if there is reason to suspect a delay or disability

least restrictive environment (LRE): the educational setting that allows a child, to the maximum extent possible, to be educated with his same-age peers who do not have disabilities

natural environment: any setting a child would typically be in if she did not have a disability, such as the home or a child care center

occupational therapy: services provided by a specialist to help children develop small motor skills for writing, performing self-care routines (eating and dressing), and other tasks that use the fingers and hands. An occupational therapist might also work with a child who has sensory issues.

participation: to be part of the same classroom routines and activities with the same materials as children without disabilities; includes physical and communication participation

physical therapy: services provided by a specialist to help children develop large motor skills, balance, and coordination so children can move as independently as possible

people-first language: a way of referring to an individual with a disability that focuses on the person rather than the disability (child with autism spectrum disorder)

pragmatics: the use and context of social language

progress: a child's growth and development over time, showing movement toward learning goals, standards, and IFSP/IEP goals

receptive language: understanding the words other people use

referral: a formal request to begin the early intervention or special education evaluation process; can be made by families, physicians, or teachers

response to intervention (RTI): a K–12 framework for providing children with systematic, targeted interventions before they fall so far behind academically that they qualify for special education

sensory integration therapy: a therapeutic approach designed to help a child with sensory processing issues learn to integrate and regulate sensory information; may include calming activities like deep pressure or activities that provide sensory stimulation, like spinning and bouncing

sensory processing issues: difficulty handling and responding to sensory information

service coordinator: individual assigned to assist families with accessing services and to explain and ensure their rights that are required by IDEA Part C

speech-language therapy: services provided by a specialist in speech and language skills to help children develop both expressive and receptive vocabularies

total communication: a combination of several methods of communication, such as listening, lip reading, facial expressions, gesturing, signing, and speaking

unaided communication: use of the body, including gestures, facial expressions, and hands (sign language), to communicate

universal design (UD): designing materials, products, and environments to be used by the greatest number of people without the need to adapt or change them

universal design for learning (UDL): the application of UD principles to education to proactively design curriculum and classroom practices so the greatest number of students can benefit without the need for adaptations or changes

Public Laws

Americans with Disabilities Act (ADA) of 1990 (Public Law 101-336): a civil rights law that prohibits discrimination against individuals with disabilities in employment, public services, public accommodations (including child care centers and schools), and telecommunications

Developmental Disabilities Assistance and Bill of Rights Act of 2000 (Public Law 106-402): provides financial assistance to support community-based services for individuals with developmental disabilities that promote self-determination and create opportunities to be independent and productive

Education for All Handicapped Children Act of 1975 (Public Law 94-142): outlined the educational rights of children and young adults ages 3 through 21 with disabilities as well as the rights of their families and allocated funds to states to provide children free, appropriate public education and related services

Education for All Handicapped Children Act, 1986 amendment (Public Law 99-457): expanded coverage of services to include children birth through age 2

Every Student Succeeds Act (ESSA) of 2015 (Public Law 114-95): reauthorizes the Elementary and Secondary Education Act (ESEA) of 1965, the US national education law

Individuals with Disabilities Education Act (IDEA) of 2004 (Public Law 108-446): governs how states and agencies provide early intervention and special education services to children and young adults

Rosa's Law of 2011 (Public Law 111-256): removed the terms *mental retardation* and *mentally retarded* from federal health, education, and labor policies and replaced them with *intellectual disability* and *individual with an intellectual disability*

Rehabilitation Act of 1973 (Public Law 93-112), Section 504: prohibits any program that receives federal funding assistance from discriminating against people with disabilities. Defines *disability* more broadly than IDEA.

References

AAP (American Academy of Pediatrics). 2006. "Identifying Infants and Young Children with Developmental Disorders in the Medical Home: An Algorithm for Developmental Surveillance and Screening." *Pediatrics* 118 (1): 405–420. doi:10.1542/peds.2006-1231.

AAP. 2015. "Children with Intellectual Disabilities." *HealthyChildren.org*. Last modified December 18. https://www.healthychildren.org/English/health-issues/conditions/developmental-disabilities /Pages/Intellectual-Disability.aspx.

AAP. 2016. "Warning Signs of Vision Problems in Infants and Children." *HealthyChildren.org*. Last modified July 19. https://www.healthychildren.org/English/health-issues/conditions/eyes/Pages /Warning-Signs-of-Vison-Problems-in-Children.aspx.

AAPOS (American Association for Pediatric Ophthalmology and Strabismus). 2016. "Retinopathy of Prematurity." Last modified June 15. http://www.aapos.org/terms/conditions/94.

Accardo, P.J., ed. 2007. *Neurodevelopmental Diagnosis and Treatment*. Vol. 1 of *Capute & Accardo's Neurodevelopmental Disabilities in Infancy and Childhood*. 3rd ed. Baltimore: Brookes Publishing.

ACCLPP (Advisory Committee on Childhood Lead Poisoning Prevention). 2012. *Low Level Lead Exposure Harms Children: A Renewed Call for Primary Prevention*. Report of ACCLPP. https:// www.cdc.gov/nceh/lead/acclpp/final_document_030712.pdf.

ACF (Administration for Children and Families) & NICHD (Eunice Kennedy Shriver National Institute of Child Health and Human Development). 2013. "Tips for Early Care and Education Providers: Simple Concepts to Embed in Everyday Routines." https://www.acf.hhs.gov/sites/default/files /ecd/508_tips_for_early_care_and_education_providers_april_2013.pdf.

ADDM CP Network (Autism and Developmental Disabilities Monitoring Cerebral Palsy Network). 2013. *2013 Community Report*. Report of the ADDM CP Network. Atlanta: National Center on Birth Defects and Developmental Disabilities. https://www.cdc.gov/ncbddd/cp/documents/community -report_v8_508.pdf.

AFB (American Foundation for the Blind). 2017a. "Accommodations and Modifications at a Glance: Educational Accommodations for Students Who Are Blind or Visually Impaired." Accessed March 1. http://www.afb.org/info/programs-and-services/professional-development/experts-guide /accommodations-and-modifications-at-a-glance/1235.

AFB. 2017b. "What Is Braille?" Accessed April 4. http://www.afb.org/info/living-with-vision-loss /braille/what-is-braille/123.

APA (American Psychiatric Association). 2013. *Diagnostic and Statistical Manual of Mental Disorders*. 5th ed. (DSM-5). Arlington, VA: APA.

ASHA (American Speech-Language-Hearing Association). 2017a. "Causes of Hearing Loss in Children." Accessed March 15. http://www.asha.org/public/hearing/disorders/causes.htm.

ASHA. 2017b. "Child Speech and Language." Accessed March 24. http://www.asha.org/public/speech /disorders/ChildSandL.htm.

ASHA. 2017c. "How Does Your Child Hear and Talk?" Accessed March 15. http://www.asha.org/public /speech/development/chart.

ASHA. 2017d. "Intellectual Disability." Accessed March 25. http://www.asha.org/PRPSpecificTopic. aspx?folderid=8589942540.

ASHA. 2017e. "Pragmatic Language Tips." Accessed March 24. http://www.asha.org/public/speech /development/PragmaticLanguageTips.

Astramovich, R.L., C. Lyons, & N.J. Hamilton. 2015. "Play Therapy for Children With Intellectual Disabilities." *Journal of Child and Adolescent Counseling* 1 (1): 27–36.

Autism Speaks. 2012. *2012 Annual Report*. Report of Autism Speaks. New York: Autism Speaks. http://www.autismspeaks.org/sites/default/files/documents/autism_speaks_2012_annual_report.pdf.

Autism Speaks. 2017. "Learn the Signs of Autism." Accessed March 21. https://www.autismspeaks.org/what-autism/learn-signs.

Balu, R., P. Zhu, F. Doolittle, E. Schiller, J. Jenkins, & R. Gersten. 2015. *Evaluation of Response to Intervention Practices for Elementary School Reading*. Report prepared for the Institute of Education Sciences (NCEE 2016-4000). Washington, DC: US Department of Education.

Bardige, B.S. 2016. *Talk to Me, Baby!: How You Can Support Young Children's Language Development*. 2nd ed. Baltimore: Brookes Publishing.

Barton, E.E. 2015. "Teaching Generalized Pretend Play and Related Behaviors to Young Children With Disabilities." *Exceptional Children* 81 (4): 489–506. doi:10.1177/0014402914563694.

Basu-Zharku, I.O. 2011. "Effects of Collectivistic and Individualistic Cultures on Imagination Inflation in Eastern and Western Cultures." *Inquiries* 3 (2): 1–5.

Bhatia, R. 2016. "Rule Out These Causes of Inattention Before Diagnosing ADHD." *Current Psychiatry* 15 (10): 32–33.

BIAA (Brain Injury Association of America). 2017. "Brain Injury in Children." Accessed March 1. http://www.biausa.org/brain-injury-children.htm.

Bolyn, M. "ADHD and Hyperactivity." *Livestrong.com*, August 10, 2015. http://www.livestrong.com/article/138332-adhd-impulsivity.

Bottema-Beutel, K., E. Turiel, M.N. DeWitt, & P.J. Wolfberg. 2017. "To Include or Not to Include: Evaluations and Reasoning About the Failure to Include Peers With Autism Spectrum Disorder in Elementary Students." *Autism* 21 (1): 51–60.

Bouck, E.C., S. Flanagan, B. Miller, & L. Bassette. 2012. "Technology in Action: Rethinking Everyday Technology as Assistive Technology to Meet Students' IEP Goals." *Journal of Special Education Technology* 27 (4): 47–57.

CAST (Center for Applied Special Technology). 2011. *Universal Design for Learning Guidelines*. Version 2.0. Wakefield, MA: CAST. http://www.udlcenter.org/sites/udlcenter.org/files/updateguidelines2_0.pdf.

Castro, D., B. Ayankoya, & C. Kasprzak. 2011. *New Voices, Nuevas Voces: Guide to Cultural and Linguistic Diversity in Early Childhood*. Baltimore: Brookes Publishing.

CDC (Centers for Disease Control and Prevention). 2015a. "Developmental Disabilities." Last modified July 9. https://www.cdc.gov/ncbddd/developmentaldisabilities/facts.html.

CDC. 2015b. "Frequently Asked Questions About Thimerosal." Last modified August 28. https://www.cdc.gov/vaccinesafety/concerns/thimerosal/faqs.html.

CDC. 2015c. "Hearing Loss in Children: Facts." Last modified October 23. https://www.cdc.gov/ncbddd/hearingloss/facts.html.

CDC. 2016a. "Autism and Developmental Disabilities Monitoring (ADDM) Network." Last modified December 5. https://www.cdc.gov/ncbddd/autism/addm.html.

CDC. 2016b. "Facts About ASD." Last modified March 28. https://www.cdc.gov/ncbddd/autism/facts.html.

CDC. 2017a. "Developmental Monitoring and Screening." Last modified February 14. https://www.cdc.gov/ncbddd/childdevelopment/screening.html.

CDC. 2017b. "Download Materials." Last modified March 21. https://www.cdc.gov/ncbddd/actearly/downloads.html.

Center for Parent Information and Resources. 2014a. "Early Intervention, Then and Now." Last modified March 15. http://www.parentcenterhub.org/repository/ei-history.

Center for Parent Information and Resources. 2014b. "Overview of Early Intervention." Last modified March 15. http://www.parentcenterhub.org/repository/ei-overview.

Center for Parent Information and Resources. 2015. "Intellectual Disability." Last modified July 15. http://www.parentcenterhub.org/repository/intellectual.

Center for Parent Information and Resources. 2016a. "Supports, Modifications, and Accommodations for Students." Last modified February 15. http://www.parentcenterhub.org/repository/accommodations.

Center for Parent Information and Resources. 2016b. "Writing the IFSP for Your Child." Last modified September 15. http://www.parentcenterhub.org/repository/ifsp.

The Center for Universal Design. 1997. *The Principles of Universal Design*. Version 2.0. Raleigh: North Carolina State University. https://www.ncsu.edu/ncsu/design/cud/about_ud/udprinciplestext.htm.

Center on the Developing Child. 2013. "InBrief: Early Childhood Mental Health." Brief. Cambridge, MA: Center on the Developing Child. http://developingchild.harvard.edu/resources/inbrief-early-childhood-mental-health.

Chazin, K.T., & J.R. Ledford. 2016. "Evidence-Based Instructional Practices for Young Children with Autism and Other Disabilities: Challenging Behavior as Communication." *Vanderbilt Kennedy Center*. Accessed March 21. http://vkc.mc.vanderbilt.edu/ebip/challenging-behavior-as-communication.

Chen, X. 2009. "Culture and Early Socio-Emotional Development." In *Encyclopedia on Early Childhood Development: Culture*, e6–e10. QC, Canada: Centre of Excellence for Early Childhood Development & Strategic Knowledge Cluster on Early Child Development. http://www.child-encyclopedia.com/sites/default/files/dossiers-complets/en/culture.pdf.

Child Care Law Center. 2011. "United States Department of Justice ADA Settlement Summaries." http://childcarelaw.org/wp-content/uploads/2014/06/DOJ-ADA-Settlement-Summaries.pdf.

Child Mind Institute. 2017a. "How Sensory Processing Issues Affect Kids in School." Accessed March 26. https://childmind.org/article/how-sensory-processing-issues-affect-kids-in-school.

Child Mind Institute. 2017b. "Quick Facts on Sensory Processing." Accessed March 26. https://childmind.org/article/quick-facts-on-sensory-processing.

Child Mind Institute. 2017c. "Sensory Processing FAQ." Accessed March 26. https://childmind.org/article/sensory-processing-faq.

Cleveland Clinic. 2013. "Attention Deficit Hyperactivity Disorder (ADHD): Stimulant Therapy." Last modified January 23. http://my.clevelandclinic.org/health/articles/attention-deficit-hyperactivity-disorder-stimulant-therapy.

CNDD (Cerebra Centre for Neurodevelopmental Disorders). 2012. *Is the Diagnosis of a Genetic Disorder Important for Children with Intellectual Disability?* Report of CNDD. Birmingham, UK: CNDD. http://www.birmingham.ac.uk/Documents/college-les/psych/cerebra/Diagnosis-in-genetic-disorders.pdf.

Conn-Powers, M., A.F. Cross, E.K. Traub, & L. Hutter-Pishgahi. 2006. "The Universal Design of Early Education: Moving Forward for All Children." *Beyond the Journal: Young Children on the Web* (September): 1–9.

Contie, V. "Learning to Diagnose Autism Spectrum Disorders." *National Institutes of Health*, July 17, 2007. https://www.nih.gov/news-events/nih-research-matters/learning-diagnose-autism-spectrum-disorders.

Cooper, J.L., R. Masi, & J. Vick. 2009. "Social-Emotional Development in Early Childhood: What Every Policymaker Should Know." Brief. New York: National Center for Children in Poverty. http://www.nccp.org/publications/pdf/text_882.pdf.

Copple, C., & S. Bredekamp, eds. 2009. *Developmentally Appropriate Practice in Early Childhood Programs Serving Children from Birth through Age 8*. 3rd ed. Washington, DC: NAEYC.

Cortiella, C., & S.H. Horowitz. 2014. *The State of Learning Disabilities: Facts, Trends and Emerging Issues*. 3rd ed. Report of the National Center for Learning Disabilities (NCLD). New York: NCLD.

Crais, E.R., L. Watson, & G. Baranek. 2009. "Use of Gesture Development in Profiling Children's Prelinguistic Communication Skills. *American Journal of Speech-Language Pathology* 18 (1): 95–108. doi:10.1044/1058-0360(2008/07-0041).

DEC (Division for Early Childhood). 2014. *DEC Recommended Practices*. https://divisionearlychildhood.egnyte.com/dl/tgv6GUXhVo.

DEC. 2017. "Division for Early Childhood." Accessed March 15. http://www.dec-sped.org.

DEC & NAEYC. 2009. "Early Childhood Inclusion." Joint position statement. Chapel Hill: The University of North Carolina, FPG Child Development Institute.

Dockrell, J., G. Lindsay, O. Palikara, & M.-A. Cullen. 2007. *Raising the Achievements of Children and Young People with Specific Speech and Language Difficulties and other Special Educational Needs through School to Work and College*. Report of the Department of Education and Skills. London, UK: Institute of Education, University of London. http://dera.ioe.ac.uk/7860/1/Dockrell2007raising.pdf.

Donahue, S.P., E.G. Buckley, S.P. Christiansen, O.A. Cruz, & L.R. Dagi. 2014. "Difficult Problems: Strabismus." *Journal of American Association for Pediatric Ophthalmology and Strabismus* 18 (4): e41. doi:10.1016/j.jaapos.2014.07.132.

Dotson-Renta, L.N. "Why Young Kids Learn Through Movement." *The Atlantic*, May 19, 2016. https://www.theatlantic.com/education/archive/2016/05/why-young-kids-learn-through-movement/483408.

ED (United States Department of Education). 2008. *Identifying and Treating Attention Deficit Hyperactivity Disorder: A Resource for School and Home*. Report of the Ed Office of Special Education and Rehabilitative Services and Office of Special Education Programs. Washington, DC: ED. https://www2.ed.gov/rschstat/research/pubs/adhd/adhd-identifying-2008.pdf.

Eisenberg, B. "5 Ways to Encourage Communication with a Non Verbal Child Diagnosed with Autism." *Friendship Circle* (blog), April 21, 2015. http://www.friendshipcircle.org/blog/2015/04/21/5-ways-to-encourage-communication-with-a-non-verbal-child-diagnosed-with-autism.

Espinosa, L. 2013. "Challenging Common Myths About Dual Language Learners: An Update to the Seminal 2008 Report." *PreK-3rd Policy to Action Brief*. No. 10. New York: Foundation for Child Development. https://www.fcd-us.org/assets/2016/04/Challenging-Common-Myths-Update.pdf.

Ferreira, J.M., M. Mäkinen, & K.S. Amorim. 2016. "Intellectual Disability in Kindergarten: Possibilities of Development Through Pretend Play." *Procedia - Social and Behavioral Sciences* 217 (2016): 487–500. doi:10.1016/j.sbspro.2016.02.024.

Filipek P.A., P.J. Accardo, S. Ashwal, G.T. Baranek, E.H. Cook, Jr., G. Dawson, B. Gordon, J.S. Gravel, C.P. Johnson, R.J. Kallen, S.E. Levy, N.J. Minshew, S. Ozonoff, B.M. Prizant, I. Rapin, S.J. Rogers, W.L. Stone, S.W. Teplin, R.F. Tuchman, & F.R. Volkmar. 2000. "Practice Parameter: Screening and Diagnosis of Autism: Report of the Quality Standards Subcommittee of the American Academy of Neurology and the Child Neurology Society." *Neurology* 55 (4): 468–479.

Flink, D. 2014. *Thinking Differently: An Inspiring Guide for Parents of Children with Learning Disabilities*. New York: William Morrow.

Fox, L., & R.H. Lentini. 2006. "'You Got It!' Teaching Social and Emotional Skills." *Beyond the Journal: Young Children on the Web* (November): 1–7.

Gasser, L., T. Malti, & A. Buholzer. 2014. "Swiss Children's Moral and Psychological Judgments About Inclusion and Exclusion of Children With Disabilities." *Child Development* 85 (2): 532–548.

Gerber, R.J., T. Wilks, & C. Erdie-Lalena. 2010. "Developmental Milestones: Motor Development." *Pediatrics in Review* 31 (7): 267–276.

Giangreco, M.F. 2010. "One-to-One Paraprofessionals for Students With Disabilities in Inclusive Classrooms: Is Conventional Wisdom Wrong?" *Intellectual and Developmental Disabilities* 48 (1): 1–13.

Giangreco, M.F. 2013. "Teacher Assistant Supports in Inclusive Schools: Research, Practices, and Alternatives." *Australasian Journal of Special Education* 37 (2): 93–106.

Green, K.B., N.P. Terry, & P.A. Gallagher. 2014. "Progress in Language and Literacy Skills Among Children With Disabilities in Inclusive Early Reading First Classrooms." *Topics in Early Childhood Special Education* 33 (4): 249–259.

Gupta, S.S., W.R. Henninger, & M.E. Vinh. 2014. *First Steps to Preschool Inclusion: How to Jumpstart Your Programwide Plan*. Baltimore: Brookes Publishing.

Gutierrez-Clellen, V., G. Simon-Cereijido, & C. Wagner. 2008. "Bilingual Children with Language Impairment: A Comparison with Monolinguals and Second Language Learners." *Applied Psycholinguistics* 29 (1): 3–20.

Hamblin, J. "Exercise Is ADHD Medication." *The Atlantic*, September 29, 2014. http://www.theatlantic.com/health/archive/2014/09/exercise-seems-to-be-beneficial-to-children/380844.

Hansen, S.N., D.E. Schendel, & E.T. Parner. 2014. "Explaining the Increase in the Prevalence of Autism Spectrum Disorders: The Proportion Attributable to Changes in Reporting Practices." *Journals of the American Medical Association Pediatrics* 169 (1): 56–62. doi:10.1001/jamapediatrics.2014.1893.

Hart B., & T.R. Risley. 1995. *Meaningful Differences in the Everyday Experience of Young American Children*. Baltimore: Brookes Publishing.

Hayes, J.A., & T. Arriola. 2005. "Pediatric Spinal Injuries." *Pediatric Nursing* 31 (6): 464–467.

Haynes, J. 2007. *Getting Started with English Language Learners: How Educators Can Meet the Challenge*. Alexandria, VA: Association for Supervision and Curriculum Development.

Heward, W.L. 2012. *Exceptional Children: An Introduction to Special Education*. 10th ed. Upper Saddle River, NJ: Pearson.

HHS (United States Department of Health and Human Services) & ED (United States Department of Education). 2015. "Policy Statement on Inclusion of Children with Disabilities in Early Childhood Programs." Joint policy statement. Washington, DC: HHS & ED. https://www2.ed.gov/policy/speced/guid/earlylearning/joint-statement-full-text.pdf.

Hillman, C.H., M.B. Pontifex, D.M. Castelli, N.A. Khan, L.B. Raine, M.R. Scudder, E.S. Drollette, R.D. Moore, C.-T.Wu, & K. Kamijo. 2014. "Effects of the FITKids Randomized Controlled Trial on Executive Control and Brain Function." *Pediatrics* 134 (4): 1062–1071.

Hitchcock, C., A. Meyer, D. Rose, & R. Jackson. 2002. "Access, Participation, and Progress in the General Curriculum." Technical brief. Wakefield, MA: National Center on Accessing the General Curriculum.

Hoff, E. 2006. "How Social Contexts Support and Shape Language Development." *Developmental Review* 26 (1): 55–88.

Hunt, E. 2011. *Human Intelligence*. New York: Cambridge University Press.

Jung, L.A. 2003. "More Better: Maximizing Natural Learning Opportunities." *Young Exceptional Children* 6 (3): 21–26.

Jung, L.A. 2007. "Writing Individualized Family Service Plan Strategies That Fit Into the ROUTINE." *Young Exceptional Children* 10 (3): 21–27.

Kane, J. "Five Misconceptions About Learning Disabilities." *PBS NewsHour*, March 16, 2012. http://www.pbs.org/newshour/rundown/five-misconceptions-about-learning-disabilities.

Kaufman, L., M. Ayub, & J.B. Vincent. 2010. "The Genetic Basis of Non-Syndromic Intellectual Disability: A Review." *Journal of Neurodevelopmental Disorders* 2 (4): 182–209.

Kellogg Eye Center. 2017. "Low Vision and Visual Rehabilitation." Accessed February 15. http://www
.umkelloggeye.org/conditions-treatments/lowvision.

Kena, G., W. Hussar, J. McFarland, C. de Brey, L. Musu-Gillette, X. Wang, J. Zhang, A. Rathbun, S.
Wilkinson-Flicker, M. Diliberti, A. Barmer, F. Bullock Mann, & E. Dunlop Velez. 2016. *The Condition
of Education 2016*. Washington, DC: US Department of Education, National Center for Education
Statistics. https://nces.ed.gov/pubs2016/2016144.pdf.

Kennedy Krieger Institute. "Is it ADHD or Typical Toddler Behavior? Ten Early Signs of ADHD Risk in
Preschool Age Children." *Kennedy Krieger Institute*, June 28, 2012. http://www.kennedykrieger.org
/overview/news/it-adhd-or-typical-toddler-behavior-ten-early-signs-adhd-risk-preschool-age
-children.

KidsHealth. 2013. "Delayed Speech or Language Development." Last modified July 15. http://
kidshealth.org/en/parents/not-talk.html.

Kieffer, R. "Social-Emotional and Behavioral Red Flags for Toddlers and Preschoolers." *North Shore
Pediatric Therapy*, June 28, 2016. http://nspt4kids.com/social-work-2/social-emotional-and
-behavioral-red-flags-for-toddlers-and-preschoolers.

Kirkendoll, S.M. "5 Signs Your Child Might Have Vision Problems." *Michigan Health* (blog), September
6, 2016. http://healthblog.uofmhealth.org/childrens-health/5-signs-your-child-might-have-vision
-problems.

Koegel, L.K., R. Matos-Fredeen, R. Lang, & R. Koegel. 2012. "Interventions for Children With Autism
Spectrum Disorders in Inclusive School Settings." *Cognitive and Behavioral Practice* 19 (3): 2–12.

Kranowitz, C. 2016. *The Out-of-Sync Child Grows Up: Coping with Sensory Processing Disorder in the
Adolescent and Young Adult Years*. New York: TarcherPerigee.

Lawson, M. "Balance Problems in Walking Babies." *Livestrong.com*, August 31, 2015. http://www
.livestrong.com/article/258531-baby-walking-balance-problems.

LDA (Learning Disabilities Association of America). 2017. "Symptoms of Learning Disabilities."
Accessed March 29. https://ldaamerica.org/symptoms-of-learning-disabilities.

Leigh, S. "Brain's Wiring Connected to Sensory Processing Disorder." *University of California San
Francisco*, January 26, 2016. https://www.ucsf.edu/news/2016/01/401461/brains-wiring
-connected-sensory-processing-disorder.

Lentini, R., B.J. Vaughn, & L. Fox. 2005. *Creating Teaching Tools for Young Children with Challenging
Behavior*. CD-ROM. Tampa: University of South Florida. http://challengingbehavior.fmhi.usf.edu
/do/resources/teaching_tools/ttyc_toc.htm.

Livadas, G. "Deaf Education: A New Philosophy." National Technical Institute for the Deaf, November
22, 2010. http://www.ntid.rit.edu/news/deaf-education-new-philosophy.

Lum, D. 2011. *Culturally Competent Practice: A Framework for Understanding Diverse Groups and
Justice Issues*. 4th ed. Boston: Cengage Learning.

MacDonald, D.M. "Diagnosing ADHD in Toddlers." *Counseling Today*, August 27, 2015. http://
ct.counseling.org/2015/08/diagnosing-adhd-in-toddlers.

March of Dimes. 2014a. "Hearing Loss." Last modified June 15. http://www.marchofdimes.com/baby
/hearing-impairment.aspx.

March of Dimes. 2014b. "Spina Bifida." Last modified May 15. http://www.marchofdimes.org
/complications/spina-bifida.aspx.

Mayo Clinic. 2014a. "Autism Spectrum Disorder." Last modified June 3. http://www.mayoclinic.org
/diseases-conditions/autism-spectrum-disorder/basics/causes/con-20021148.

Mayo Clinic. 2014b. "Dyslexia." Last modified August 8. http://www.mayoclinic.org/diseases
-conditions/dyslexia/basics/definition/con-20021904.

Mayo Clinic. 2016a. "Attention-Deficit/Hyperactivity Disorder (ADHD) in Children." Last modified March 11. http://www.mayoclinic.org/diseases-conditions/adhd/symptoms-causes/dxc-20196181.

Mayo Clinic. 2016b. "Lead Poisoning." Last modified December 6. http://www.mayoclinic.org/diseases-conditions/lead-poisoning/symptoms-causes/dxc-20275054.

Mayo Clinic. 2016c. "What Are the Signs of Learning Disorders?" Last modified February 10. http://www.mayoclinic.org/healthy-lifestyle/childrens-health/in-depth/learning-disorders/art-20046105?pg=2.

McLeod, S., G. Daniel, & B. Barr. 2013. "'When He's Around His Brothers…He's Not So Quiet': The Private and Public Worlds of School-aged Children with Speech Sound Disorder." *Journal of Communication Disorders* 46 (1): 70–83.

McWilliam, R.A. & A.M. Casey. 2008. *Engagement of Every Child in the Preschool Classroom.* Baltimore: Brookes Publishing.

McWilliam, R.A. & S. Scott. 2001. "Integrating Therapy into the Classroom." *Individualizing Inclusion in Child Care*, 1–6. https://www.uvm.edu/~cdci/iteam/documents/IntegratingTherapyIntoClassrooms1.pdf.

MDA (Muscular Dystrophy Association). 2017. "Duchenne Muscular Dystrophy (DMD)." Accessed February 23. https://www.mda.org/disease/duchenne-muscular-dystrophy.

Mellon, N.K., J.K. Niparko, C. Rathmann, G. Mathur, T. Humphries, D.J. Napoli, T. Handley, S. Scambler, & J.D. Lantos. 2015. "Should All Deaf Children Learn Sign Language?" *Pediatrics* 136 (1): 170–176. doi:10.1542/peds.2014-1632.

Meyer, A., D.H. Rose, & D. Gordon. 2014. *Universal Design for Learning: Theory and Practice.* Wakefield, MA: CAST.

NAC (National Autism Center). 2015. *Findings and Conclusions: National Standards Project, Phase 2: Addressing the Need for Evidence-Based Practice Guidelines for Autism Spectrum Disorder.* Report of NAC, a Center of May Institute. Randolph, MA: NAC.

NAEYC. 2009. "Developmentally Appropriate Practice in Early Childhood Programs Serving Children Birth through Age 8." Position statement. Washington, DC: NAEYC.

NAEYC. 2016. *Code of Ethical Conduct and Statement of Commitment.* Brochure. Rev. ed. Washington, DC: NAEYC.

NASET (National Association of Special Education Teachers). 2017. "Introduction to Learning Disabilities." Accessed March 29. http://www.naset.org/2522.0.html.

NCBDDD (National Center on Birth Defects and Developmental Disabilities). 2017. "Facts About Vision Loss." Accessed February 15. https://www.cdc.gov/ncbddd/actearly/pdf/parents_pdfs/visionlossfactsheet.pdf.

NEI (National Eye Institute). 2017. "Common Vision Problems." Accessed March 20. https://nei.nih.gov/healthyeyes/problems.

Neidert, P.L., G.W. Rooker, M.W. Bayles, & J.R. Miller. 2013. "Functional Analysis of Problem Behavior." In *Handbook of Crisis Intervention and Developmental Disabilities*, eds. D.D. Reed, F.D. DiGennaro Reed, & J.K. Luiselli, 147–167. New York: Springer.

Nelson, F., & T. Mann. 2011. "Opportunities in Public Policy to Support Early Childhood Mental Health: The Role of Psychologists and Policymakers." *American Psychologist* 66 (2): 129–139.

Nemeth, K.N. 2009. *Many Languages, One Classroom: Teaching Dual and English Language Learners.* Beltsville, MD: Gryphon House.

NICHD (Eunice Kennedy Shriver National Institute of Child Health and Human Development). 2017a. "How Many People are Affected/At Risk for Learning Disabilities?" Accessed March 26. https://www.nichd.nih.gov/health/topics/learning/conditioninfo/pages/risk.aspx.

NICHD. 2017b. "What Causes Learning Disabilities?" Accessed March 26. https://www.nichd.nih.gov /health/topics/learning/conditioninfo/pages/causes.aspx.

NIDCD (National Institute on Deafness and Other Communication Disorders). 2017a. "Cochlear Implants." Last modified March 6. https://www.nidcd.nih.gov/health/cochlear-implants.

NIDCD. 2017b. "Hearing Aids." Last modified March 6. https://www.nidcd.nih.gov/health/hearing -aids.

NIDCD. 2017c. "Speech and Language Developmental Milestones." Last modified March 6. https:// www.nidcd.nih.gov/health/speech-and-language.

NIMH (National Institute of Mental Health). 2008. *National Institute of Mental Health Strategic Plan.* Washington, DC: NIMH.

NIMH. 2016. "Autism Spectrum Disorder." Last modified October 15. https://www.nimh.nih.gov /health/topics/autism-spectrum-disorders-asd/index.shtml.

NINDS (National Institute of Neurological Disorders and Stroke). 2015. *Autism Spectrum Disorder.* Brochure. Bethesda, MD: NINDS. https://catalog.ninds.nih.gov/pubstatic//15-1877/15-1877.pdf.

NJCLD (National Joint Committee on Learning Disabilities). 2010. "Comprehensive Assessment and Evaluation of Students with Learning Disabilities." *Learning Disability Quarterly* 34 (1): 3–16.

Padden, C.A., & T. Humphries. 2006. *Inside Deaf Culture.* Cambridge, MA: Harvard University Press.

Pakula, A.T., K. Van Naarden Braun, M. Yeargin-Allsopp. 2009. "Cerebral Palsy: Classification and Epidemiology." *Physical Medicine and Rehabilitation Clinics of North America* 20 (3): 425–452.

Palmer, B. "Get Ready for the Next Big Medical Fight: Is Sensory Processing Disorder a Real Disease?" *Slate*, February 27, 2014. http://www.slate.com/articles/health_and_science/medical _examiner/2014/02/sensory_processing_disorder_the_debate_over_whether_spd_is_a_real _disease.html.

Paradis, J. 2010. "The Interface Between Bilingual Development and Specific Language Impairment." *Applied Psycholinguistics* 31 (2): 227–252.

Paradis, J., F. Genesee, & M.B. Crago. 2011. *Dual Language Development and Disorders: A Handbook on Bilingualism and Second Language Learning.* 2nd ed. Baltimore: Brookes Publishing.

Passman, R. H. 1977. "Providing Attachment Objects to Facilitate Learning and Reduce Distress: Effects of Mothers and Security Blankets." *Developmental Psychology* 13 (1): 25–28.

Peters, S. 2004. "Inclusive Education: An EFA Strategy for All Children." Working paper. Washington, DC: World Bank.

Prelock, P.A., T. Hutchins, & F.P. Glascoe. 2008. "Speech-Language Impairment: How to Identify the Most Common and Least Diagnosed Disability of Childhood." *The Medscape Journal of Medicine* 10 (6): 136. https://www.ncbi.nlm.nih.gov/pmc/articles/PMC2491683.

Raising Children Network. 2016. "Signs of Autism Spectrum Disorder in Older Children and Teenagers." Last modified September 21. http://raisingchildren.net.au/articles/autism_spectrum_disorder _signs_teenagers.html.

Ray, J.A., J. Pewitt-Kinder, & S. George. 2009. "Partnering with Parents of Children with Special Needs." *Young Children* 64 (5):16–23.

Reynolds, S., S.J. Lane, & C. Gennings. 2009. "The Moderating Role of Sensory Overresponsivity in HPA Activity: A Pilot Study with Children Diagnosed with ADHD." *Journal of Attention Disorders* 13 (5): 468–478. doi:10.1177/1087054708329906.

Roman-Lantzy, C. 2007. *Cortical Visual Impairment: An Approach to Assessment and Intervention.* New York: AFB Press.

Romski, M., R.A. Sevcik, L.B. Adamson, M. Cheslock, A. Smith, R.M. Barker, & R. Bakeman. 2010. "Randomized Comparison of Augmented and Non-Augmented Language Interventions for Toddlers with Developmental Delays and Their Parents." *Journal of Speech, Language, and Hearing Research* 53 (2): 350–364.

Rose, D.H., & A. Meyer, eds. 2006. *A Practical Reader in Universal Design for Learning.* Cambridge, MA: Harvard Education Press.

RTI Action Network. 2017. "What is RTI?" Accessed March 26. http://www.rtinetwork.org/learn/what.

Rubin, K.H., & M. Menzer. 2010. "Culture and Social Development." In *Encyclopedia on Early Childhood Development: Culture,* e1–e8. QC, Canada: Centre of Excellence for Early Childhood Development & Strategic Knowledge Cluster on Early Child Development. http://www.child -encyclopedia.com/sites/default/files/textes-experts/en/601/culture-and-social-development.pdf.

Rutherford, G. 2011. "'Doing Right By' Teacher Aides, Students with Disabilities, and Relational Social Justice." *Harvard Educational Review* 81 (Spring): 95–118.

Samuels, C.A. "What Are Multitiered Systems of Supports?" *Education Week,* December 13, 2016. http://www.edweek.org/ew/articles/2016/12/14/what-are-multitiered-systems-of-supports.html.

Sandall, S.R., & I.S. Schwartz. 2008. *Building Blocks for Teaching Preschoolers with Special Needs.* 2nd ed. Baltimore: Brookes Publishing.

Schick, B. 2011. "The Development of American Sign Language and Manually Coded English Systems." In Vol. 1 of *The Oxford Handbook of Deaf Studies, Language, and Education,* 2nd ed., eds. M. Marschark & P.E. Spencer, 229–240. New York: Oxford University Press.

Severns, M. 2012. "Starting Early With English Language Learners: First Lessons From Illinois." Policy paper. Washington, DC: New America Foundation.

Sholtis, S. "Increasing Prevalence of Autism is Due, in Part, to Changing Diagnoses." *Penn State Science,* July 22, 2015. http://science.psu.edu/news-and-events/2015-news/Girirajan7-2015.

Snyder, P., M.L. Hemmeter, S. Sandall, & M. McLean. 2007. *Impact of Professional Development on Preschool Teachers' Use of Embedded-Instruction Practices.* Grant awarded by the Institute of Education Sciences (Project No. R324A070008). Washington, DC: US Department of Education.

Sparks, S.D. "Study: RTI Practice Falls Short of Promise." *Education Week,* November 6, 2015. http:// www.edweek.org/ew/articles/2015/11/11/study-rti-practice-falls-short-of-promise.html?cmp=eml -eb-pop112415web.

SPD Support. 2017. "SPD Symptoms Checklist." Accessed March 1. http://spdsupport.org/resources /symptoms.shtml.

Spear-Swerling, L. "Learning Disabilities in English Language Learners." *LD OnLine,* February 1, 2006. http://www.ldonline.org/spearswerling/Learning_Disabilities_in_English_Language_Learners.

Stokoe, W.C., Jr., D.C. Casterline, & C.G. Croneberg. 1965. *A Dictionary of American Sign Language on Linguistic Principles.* Washington, DC: Gallaudet College Press.

Strain, P.S., & E.H. Bovey. 2011. "Randomized, Controlled Trial of the LEAP Model of Early Intervention for Young Children With Autism Spectrum Disorders." *Topics in Early Childhood Special Education* 31 (3): 133–154.

Subcommittee on ADHD (Subcommittee on Attention-Deficit/Hyperactivity Disorder, Steering Committee on Quality Improvement and Management). 2011. "ADHD: Clinical Practice Guideline for the Diagnosis, Evaluation, and Treatment of Attention-Deficit/Hyperactivity Disorder in Children and Adolescents." *Pediatrics* 128 (5): 1007–1022.

Syracuse University Disability Cultural Center. 2012. "An Introductory Guide to Disability Language and Empowerment." http://sudcc.syr.edu/LanguageGuide.

Tabors, P.O. 2008. *One Child, Two Languages: A Guide for Early Childhood Educators of Children Learning English as a Second Language*. 2nd ed. Baltimore: Brookes Publishing.

TACSEI (Technical Assistance Center on Social Emotional Intervention for Young Children). 2011. "The Process of Positive Behavior Support (PBS): Step Three, Functional Behavioral Assessment." Accessed March 24. http://challengingbehavior.fmhi.usf.edu/explore/pbs/step3_function.htm.

Taylor, L.E., A.L. Swerdfeger, & G.D. Eslick. 2014. "Vaccines Are Not Associated With Autism: An Evidence-Based Meta-Analysis of Case-Control and Cohort Studies." *Vaccine* 32 (29): 3623–3629.

TCDD (Texas Council for Developmental Disabilities). 2013. "Section I: Basic Behavior Components (A-B-C Model)." ProjectIDEAL. Accessed March 24. http://www.projectidealonline.org/v/basic-behavior-components.

UNICEF (United Nations Children's Fund). 2009. *The State of the World's Children Special Edition: Celebrating 20 Years of the Convention on the Rights of the Child*. New York: UNICEF.

UNICEF (United Nations Children's Fund), WHO (World Health Organization), UNESCO (United Nations Educational, Scientific and Cultural Organization), UNFPA (United Nations Population Fund), UNDP (United Nations Development Programme), UNAIDS (Joint United Nations Programme on HIV/AIDS), WFP (World Food Programme), & The World Bank. 2010. *Facts for Life*. 4th ed. New York: UNICEF, WHO, UNESCO, UNFPA, UNDP, UNAIDS, WFP & The World Bank. http://www.factsforlifeglobal.org/resources/factsforlife-en-full.pdf.

Van Naarden Braun, K., N. Doernberg, L. Schieve, D. Christensen, A. Goodman, & M. Yeargin-Allsopp. 2016. "Birth Prevalence of Cerebral Palsy: A Population-Based Study." *Pediatrics* 137 (1): 1–9.

Vann, M.R. 2011. "Mental Illness in Kids: The Surprising Warning Signs." *Everyday Health*. Last modified May 18. http://www.everydayhealth.com/emotional-health/mental-illness-in-kids-surprising-warning-signs.aspx.

The Vision Council. 2017. "Potential Problems and Warning Signs." Accessed February 15. https://www.thevisioncouncil.org/content/potential-problems-warning-signs/kids.

Visser, S.N., R.H. Bitsko, M.L. Danielson, R.M. Ghandour, S.J. Blumberg, L.A. Schieve, J.R. Holbrook, M.L. Wolraich, & S.P. Cuffe. 2015. "Treatment of Attention-Deficit/Hyperactivity Disorder Among Children with Special Health Care Needs." *Journal of Pediatrics* 166 (6): 1423–1430.

Wadman, R., K. Durkin, & G. Conti-Ramsden. 2011. "Close Relationships in Adolescents With and Without a History of Specific Language Impairment." *Language, Speech, and Hearing Services in Schools* 42 (1): 41–51.

Washington State Office of Superintendent of Public Instruction (OSPI). 2008. *A Guide to Assessment in Early Childhood: Infancy to Age Eight*. Tacoma: Washington State OSPI. http://www.k12.wa.us/EarlyLearning/pubdocs/assessment_print.pdf.

WHO (World Health Organization). 2010. *Exposure to Lead: A Major Public Health Concern*. Report of WHO. Geneva, Switzerland: WHO. http://www.who.int/ipcs/features/lead.pdf.

Winton, P.J. 2016. "Taking Stock and Moving Forward: Implementing Quality Early Childhood Inclusive Practices." In *Handbook of Early Childhood Special Education*, eds. B. Reichow, B.A. Boyd, E.E. Barton, & S.L. Odom, 57–74. Cham, Switzerland: Springer International Publishing.

YCDC (The Yale Center for Dyslexia and Creativity). 2017. "I Have Dyslexia. What Does It Mean?" Accessed March 26. http://dyslexia.yale.edu/whatisdyslexia.html.

Zembar, M.J., & L.B. Blume. 2009. *Middle Childhood Development: A Contextual Approach*. Upper Saddle River, NJ: Pearson.

Resources

Organizations and Online Resources

American Council on Rural Special Education (ACRES): provides services and information for individuals with disabilities living in rural areas. http://acres-sped.org

American Speech-Language-Hearing Association (ASHA): professional organization for specialists in the speech, language, and hearing fields; provides resources for the public on understanding communication and communication disorders. http://www.asha.org

The Arc: national, community-based organization that provides programs and advocates for individuals with intellectual and developmental disabilities (previously known as National Association for Retarded Citizens; Association for Retarded Citizens of the United States). http://www.thearc.org

Autism Society: grassroots organization formed to increase public awareness about individuals with autism, advocate for better services, and share the latest research on treatments and educational approaches. http://www.autism-society.org

Brain Injury Association of America (BIAA): advocacy group that provides information on brain injuries, including research on prevention and treatment. http://www.biausa.org

Center on the Social and Emotional Foundations for Early Learning (CSEFEL): promotes the social and emotional development and school readiness of children birth to age 5; offers information for families, teachers, and trainers. http://csefel.vanderbilt.edu

Children and Adults with Attention-Deficit/Hyperactivity Disorder (CHADD): provides the most current research and information about advocacy and best practices in educating individuals with ADHD. http://www.chadd.org

Council for Exceptional Children (CEC): professional organization for educators of students with disabilities. http://www.cec.sped.org

Disability Resource Community (DRC): a nonprofit organization that offers resources to help people with disabilities and their families become advocates and active members of the community. http://www.disabilityresource.org

Division for Early Childhood (DEC) of the Council for Exceptional Children: professional membership organization for early childhood special education teachers and families of young children with disabilities that promotes the use of evidence-based practices. http://www.dec-sped.org

Early Childhood Technical Assistance Center (ECTA Center): provides information related to the early childhood provisions of IDEA to increase the implementation of effective practices and enhance outcomes for young children. http://ectacenter.org

Exceptional Parent (eParent): website and magazine with practical advice for parents and families of children and adults with disabilities. http://www.eparent.com

International Dyslexia Association (IDA): professional organization that provides information and resources for those with dyslexia and for teachers and parents. https://dyslexiaida.org

Military Families Early Intervention Team: part of the Military Families Learning Network's (MFLN) Family Development team, seeks to enhance the capacity of professionals working with military families who have a young child with a developmental delay or disability. https://militaryfamilies.extension.org/2015/03/18/welcome-to-the-ei-concentration-area-blog

National Association of the Deaf (NAD): provides information about best practices for teaching children with hearing loss. http://www.nad.org

National Association of Special Education Teachers (NASET): membership organization for special education teachers that provides support and best practices to help teachers be successful. http://www.naset.org

National Center for Learning Disabilities (NCLD): provides information to parents and teachers about learning disabilities to improve awareness and transform schools so every child with a learning disability can be successful. http://www.ncld.org

National Down Syndrome Society (NDSS): advocacy group for individuals with Down syndrome that provides information and best practices. http://www.ndss.org

National Federation of the Blind (NFB): advocacy group that provides the most recent research, technology, and best practices in encouraging independence and self-confidence in individuals who are blind or visually impaired. https://nfb.org

National Federation of Families for Children's Mental Health (NFFCMH): a national organization that focuses on the issues of children with emotional, behavioral, or mental health disorders. http://www.ffcmh.org

National Library Service for the Blind and Physically Handicapped (NLS): network of cooperating libraries that provides books and other materials in braille and other formats that can be read by individuals who are blind or visually impaired. http://www.loc.gov/nls

National Organization on Disability (NOD): advocacy organization that promotes the full participation of people with disabilities in all aspects of society. http://www.nod.org

Office of Special Education and Rehabilitative Services (OSERS): provides information about IDEA. https://www2.ed.gov/about/offices/list/osers/osep/osep-idea.html

TASH: promotes the full inclusion and participation of children and adults with significant disabilities in all aspects of society (previously known as The American Association for the Education of the Severely and Profoundly Handicapped; The Association for the Severely Handicapped; and The Association for Persons with Severe Handicaps). http://tash.org

Technical Assistance Center on Social Emotional Intervention for Young Children (TACSEI): offers research and practical information about improving social and emotional outcomes for young children with, or at risk for, delays or disabilities. http://challengingbehavior.fmhi.usf.edu

What Works Clearinghouse (WWC): reviews the latest research on evidence-based educational programs, products, practices, and policies; managed by the Institute of Education Sciences (IES). http://ies.ed.gov/ncee/wwc

Wrightslaw: provides information on special education, special education law, and advocacy. http://www.wrightslaw.com

Articles and Publications

Campbell, P.H., A.A. Kennedy, & S.A. Milbourne. 2012. *Cara's Kit for Toddlers: Creating Adaptations for Routines and Activities*. Baltimore: Brookes Publishing. Available from NAEYC.

Division for Early Childhood. 2014. *DEC Recommended Practices*. Division for Early Childhood, Council for Exceptional Children. http://www.dec-sped.org /dec-recommended-practices.

Milbourne, S.A., & P.H. Campbell. 2007. *Cara's Kit: Creating Adaptations for Routines and Activities*. Reston, VA: Division for Early Childhood, Council for Exceptional Children. Available from NAEYC.

US Department of Health and Human Services. 2014. "Birth to 5: Watch Me Thrive! An Early Care and Education Provider's Guide for Developmental and Behavioral Screening." https://www.acf.hhs.gov/sites/default/files/ecd/ece_providers_guide _march2014.pdf.

US Department of Health and Human Services. 2014. "Birth to 5: Watch Me Thrive! An Early Intervention and Early Childhood Special Education Provider's Guide to Support Developmental and Behavioral Screening Initiatives." https://www.acf.hhs.gov/sites /default/files/ecd/early_intervention_guide_march2014.pdf.

For Families

Each state has one or more Parent Training and Information Centers, known as PTI, that offer families resources and information on services and parent rights. Find a listing by state at http://www.parentcenterhub.org/find-your-center.

Acknowledgments

Even though my name is the only one on the cover, I do not want to give the impression that I was able to complete this extraordinary task without help. In fact, it was with a lot of help!

First and foremost, I need to thank Holly Bohart, my NAEYC editor, who was patient, kind, supportive, honest, and tough. She and Kathy Charner, the Editor in Chief, were the perfect people to guide someone through writing her first book. Thank you, thank you, thank you! I hope every first-time author has people like Holly and Kathy behind them.

Thank you to my behind-the-scenes support system at home, especially Brad for giving me the time and room to write (and for listening to me vent about it all). My cheerleaders—fellow educators and authors Karen Nemeth, Janis Strasser, and Rosanne Hansel—provided wonderful footsteps for me to follow. Paula Danzinger, my friend and mentor, kept me calm while she pushed me forward, and Juan Torres and Diane Mari gave their honest feedback on the first draft (along with a few laughs in the margin). Thank you all for everything.

A big thank-you goes to the staff and children of National Children's Center in Washington, DC, who are the stars of many of the wonderful photographs in this book. The staff's enthusiasm never waned through a long photo session, and their deep care and support for the children are evident in the photos.

Finally, I want to dedicate this book to my parents, Joan and Rudy. I love you and miss you both every day, and I wish you were here to share this with me.

About the Author

Like her mother and grandmother, Pam Brillante, EdD, knew her calling to be a teacher. Since finding her passion for special education, she has spent 30 years working as a special education teacher, administrator, consultant, and professor.

Dr. Brillante earned a bachelor of arts degree in special education from William Paterson University of New Jersey and started her career as a teacher in a K–2 self-contained special education classroom for students with multiple disabilities. She taught children in both self-contained and inclusive preschool classes in the public schools while earning a master's degree in curriculum and instruction with a concentration in early childhood education at William Paterson.

From the classroom, Dr. Brillante transitioned to almost a decade working for the New Jersey Department of Education as early childhood specialist for the Office of Special Education, helping public schools develop high-quality, inclusive early childhood programs. During this time, she earned a doctorate in educational leadership from Rowan University.

In addition to her full-time faculty position in the Department of Special Education and Professional Counseling at William Paterson, Dr. Brillante continues to consult with school districts and present to teachers and families on the topic of high-quality, inclusive early childhood practices.

An author for NAEYC and other publications, Dr. Brillante is a founder and co-facilitator of the NAEYC Early Childhood Consultants and Authors Interest Forum. She is also a consulting editor and workshop reviewer for NAEYC as well as a member of the Head Start Governance Advisory Committee for Acelaro Learning.